KT-481-374

Letters to the Home Front

Positive Thoughts and Ideas for
Parents Bringing Up Children
with Developmental Disabilities,
Particularly those with an
Autism Spectrum Disorder

John Clements

Jessica Kingsley *Publishers*
London and Philadelphia

First published in 2013
by Jessica Kingsley Publishers
116 Pentonville Road
London N1 9JB, UK
and
400 Market Street, Suite 400
Philadelphia, PA 19106, USA

www.jkp.com

Copyright © John Clements 2013

All rights reserved. No part of this publication may be reproduced in any
material form (including photocopying or storing it in any medium by electronic
means and whether or not transiently or incidentally to some other use of this
publication) without the written permission of the copyright owner except in
accordance with the provisions of the Copyright, Designs and Patents Act 1988
or under the terms of a licence issued by the Copyright Licensing Agency Ltd,
Saffron House, 6–10 Kirby Street, London EC1N 8TS. Applications for the
copyright owner's written permission to reproduce any part of this publication
should be addressed to the publisher.

Warning: The doing of an unauthorised act in relation to a copyright work may
result in both a civil claim for damages and criminal prosecution.

Library of Congress Cataloging in Publication Data
Clements, John, 1946 Dec. 1-
  Letters to the home front : positive thoughts and ideas for parents bringing up
children with
developmental disabilities, particularly those with an autism spectrum disorder /
John Clements.
     pages cm
  Includes index.
  ISBN 978-1-84905-332-7 (alk. paper)
  1. Children with autism spectrum disorders--Rehabilitation. 2. Autistic
children--Care. 3. Parents of
developmentally disabled children. I. Title.
  RJ506.A9C54 2013
  618.92'85882--dc23
                                    2012048908

British Library Cataloguing in Publication Data
A CIP catalogue record for this book is available from the British Library

ISBN 978 1 84905 332 7
eISBN 978 0 85700 678 3

Printed and bound in Great Britain

'John Clements has been a very popular and successful professional who has helped parents and caregivers over the past four decades to better understand and remediate behavioural challenges in children with ASD. This book presents a helpful, interesting and easy to read summary of this work. The format involving a series of letters between him and various constituents makes for fascinating reading and adds a note of reality. This is a pragmatic book that parents and professionals will enjoy reading and greatly appreciate because it fills many of the gaps in our understanding of ASD and how to work more successfully with these individuals on day-to-day concerns in the home, the classroom and the community.'

— *Dr Gary Mesibov, Professor Emeritus of Psychology, Departments of Psychiatry and Psychology, University of North Carolina*

'In this extremely accessible book, John Clements draws on his extensive knowledge of the problems that families of children with autism and other conditions may face, to offer much needed advice. In "user-friendly" letters, he neither preaches nor judges, but discusses in un-sensationalist terms just what those problems may involve and some of the ways that they may be tackled. His compassion and empathy are clearly evident in his approach, and, although he makes it clear that there are no magic answers, I feel sure that many families will find his words very comforting and of immense practical help.'

— *Jane Asher, President of the National Autistic Society*

'Empowering, hard-hitting, honest. *Letters to the Home Front* offers parents bringing up children with developmental/ intellectual disabilities invaluable insights, practical strategies – a wealth of information and wisdom. The author John Clements also puts forward a down to earth and realistic view of the situations many families and individuals find themselves in and with regard to accessing and receiving services from multi-disciplinary providers. Truly a book to reflect on from a multi-dimensional perspective.'

— *Sue Telkamp, mother of a young man diagnosed with ASD*

C333514278

by the same author

Transition or Transformation?
Helping Young People with Autistic Spectrum Disorder Set Out on a
Hopeful Road towards Their Adult Lives
John Clements, Julia Hardy and Stephanie Lord
ISBN 978 1 84310 964 8
eISBN 978 0 85700 386 7

People with Autism Behaving Badly
Helping People with ASD Move On from Behavioral and Emotional
Challenges
John Clements
ISBN 978 1 84310 765 1
eISBN 978 1 84642 087 0

Assessing Behaviors Regarded as Problematic
for People with Developmental Disabilities
John Clements and Neil Martin
ISBN 978 1 85302 998 1
eISBN 978 1 84642 648 3

Behavioral Concerns and Autistic Spectrum Disorders
Explanations and Strategies for Change
John Clements and Ewa Zarkowska
ISBN 978 1 85302 742 0
eISBN 978 1 84642 168 6

For Lisa and Jim, Leon and Sacha

Contents

Acknowledgements

I would like to thank all those families that I have met and worked with in the last 40 years. They have taught me so much and played a large part in gifting me a career that has brought me huge satisfaction. I hope that I have been able to give back as much as I have received. Closer to home, I would like to thank my wife Cheryl and my son Noah, who also teach me a lot, support and encourage me and put up with the disruption and grumpiness that comes with writing. Cheryl also provided very helpful comments on this manuscript. This is the last book...promise...well maybe. A special mention for Sue Telkamp, from whose conversations and insights I have benefited so much over so many years. Finally a thank you to the Jessica Kingsley team, particularly to Jessica herself, for all the encouragement and help that has been part of our working relationship over the past 15–20 years.

Introduction

Bringing up any child successfully is a great challenge for parents. Bringing up successfully a child with autism or other developmental disabilities is an even greater challenge, the size of which escalates rapidly if that child presents with long-term and serious behavioural issues. The parents who are the focus of this book face many, many serious decisions as they journey through the upbringing of their sons and daughters. Some of these are what we might call tactical decisions – for example, how to deal with a specific behaviour, whether to pursue a particular type of therapy or how to manage a conflict with a service-providing agency. Others are more strategic – for example, deciding on where your child should live, how to help the other children in the family or what should happen once you, the parents, are no longer around. Often parents have limited support in making these decisions and wonder about the quality of any advice that they are offered. This book is intended to be of help at these times of decision making. I hope that it will provide reassurance, some insights, a space for reflection and practical ideas. I see it as a kind of 'traveller's companion' to be dipped into as needed. It is most certainly not a text book, nor is it intended as a comprehensive coverage of all the issues parents face. It deals with some of the topics that have come up most frequently in my work with parents.

Beyond the parents themselves the book is also addressed to those many people paid to provide services to children with developmental disabilities. All those making their living in 'disabilityland' are absolutely dependent upon parents doing a great job if they are to achieve their own goals, whether they are teachers, psychologists, doctors, social workers or care providers of one sort or another. The success of home life is the bedrock of all our achievements. It would seem blindingly obvious that, if we are concerned about the welfare of children, young people and adults with developmental disabilities, these understandings would translate into readily available support services for their parents. Over the 40-year span of my career some progress has been made in this respect, but it remains frighteningly limited. Many parents still struggle to get help of any kind with the huge challenges they may face at home. Many who do have access to services still find themselves blamed and criticised for what is going on at home. I want those who provide services and have contact with families to have a better understanding of some of the realities of family life and the parenting process. Unless you work with parents in their own homes it is hard to imagine what family life can be like – the extraordinary lengths parents have to go to if the family is to function. There are some very vivid tales in this book that illustrate this point. I hope that this will enable people to adopt a more sympathetic approach to parents, to be a little less quick to pass judgement on parents struggling with the issues that are represented here and thereby provide more effective support to the families with whom they come into contact.

Overview of the book

The book is presented as a series of letters addressed to parents. This is a stylistic device to present communications

I have had with parents, sometimes face to face, sometimes by telephone or email. It was chosen because so often, for the parents I have worked with, 'letters home' almost always signify bad news (notification of 'bad behaviour', need for an emergency meeting, child suspended or excluded from a service). It is hoped that these letters home are rather more supportive and helpful!

The book is organised into four sections but it is important to remember that the text is meant to be dipped into as needed, not read cover to cover. All the text pieces are 'stand alone' and do not require reading in any particular order. However, to help the reader have some idea of where to look for things that are relevant I will outline briefly the content of each section.

Section 1

Bringing up a child with serious developmental disabilities is hard from many points of view. But one thing that I have often heard parents say, particularly parents of a child on the autistic spectrum, is that although they love their child they are not sure if their child regards them in any special light. The parents feel dispensable, easily replaced and often ineffective. They are not sure what and how much they mean to their child. This is not surprising as the kinds of feedback many of the children give is not direct, not synchronised with parenting input and not easily readable. Yet to me, as an outsider, I have never been in any doubt as to the central and enduring significance of the parents to the child's development and well being. Just saying this did not seem enough. So I asked three articulate young people on the autistic spectrum who had been very 'challenging' growing up, but who were moving on positively now, to write a letter to their families, to point out the things during their earlier years that they appreciated and that helped them, as well as the things that they did not find so helpful.

Section 2

Each piece in this section tries to address some of the general questions or issues that arise in the parenting process rather than the management of specific situations. They are topics that have come up frequently in my conversations with parents over the years. They are topics that permit no easy or clear-cut answers but involve very important decisions that parents may have to make.

Section 3

This contains items written in the form of letters to specific parents about the management of some very difficult behavioural issues presented in the context of 'autism'. These are all based upon actual conversations that I have had with specific families, although some details have been changed to protect confidentiality. All have been included with the agreement of the families concerned. These are conversations that may have been conducted by email, by telephone or face to face; or any combination of these forms. These conversations have sometimes taken place over a matter of weeks, sometimes over a matter of years.

Section 4

This is the contrarian section. It takes some ideas that reflect current wisdom and raises questions about those ideas, challenges those orthodoxies. It is meant to stimulate thinking through an op ed format, not to reveal hidden truths through detailed academic discussion. The point of this is to encourage parents to challenge ideas that are put to them, to consider alternative viewpoints and to request and weigh the evidence. This last point is crucial. The digital age has many virtues and the internet can be a great source of information, but in the same way that the tower of Babel was potentially a great source of language learning. There can be a fatal confound of fact and opinion and a tendency for opinions that are repeated often and with great fervency to be treated as facts. This section of the book is there to encourage the quest for facts and information so that opinion might evolve from a consideration of evidence rather than from the opinion of someone else. It is the contention here that the interests of a family are better served by this approach than by a rigid adherence to some kind of orthodoxy, whether that orthodoxy is promoted by high-status professionals or internet wackos.

Letters to my family

Three young people on the autistic spectrum reflect on their growing up

I asked three articulate young people on the autistic spectrum to reflect on their growing up and to write a letter to their parent(s) about the things that they appreciated and found helpful and the things that were problematic or that could have been done differently. Dean, Hannah and Alex responded magnificently. Hannah found the letter format did not really work for her so she has crafted something that enables her to express herself in a way that is more valid for her. What is extraordinary here is the level of awareness that these young people show about the support that they received, an awareness that would not have been obvious at all to their families at the time. At the end of each letter there are brief biographical details about each of the young people as provided by the authors themselves.

A. Dean's letter

Mum,

As you know, I speak at conferences all over the UK about my experiences of Asperger's syndrome, and the one comment I get again and again is 'Your mum must be so proud of you…' I know that you are – against the odds.

We didn't have the easiest of starts, did we? As a baby, my sleeping pattern left a lot to be desired, and it never really improved. It must have been an absolute nightmare trying to get a hyperactive six-year-old off to sleep when all he wanted to do was watch *Doctor Who* until the early hours! Eventually, you gave up work altogether and I can't help feeling like that was my fault – you sacrificed your career in order to be at home with your extremely challenging child. And challenging is definitely the word! Refusing to get in the bath, standing at the top of the stairs screeching like Kate Bush, aggressive, defiant… I don't know how you did it!

And once I was at school, things only seemed to get harder. Despite you devoting all of your time to bringing your children up, you faced accusations from professionals that my bad behaviour was down to your parenting. That must have hurt. Bringing up a child with special needs can be the most challenging job in the world, and to have been endlessly demoralised by authority figures whilst you tried to do that would be enough to crush anyone. But not you.

You may not have been an expert in Asperger's, but you were an expert in your child, and you fought tooth and nail to get me the support I needed. You knew that with the right support I could thrive in mainstream and you battled for me to remain there, despite the authorities pushing to put me in a special school. You knew special school wouldn't be right for me and you stuck to your guns. That takes guts. You were endlessly told that I'd achieve nothing and that I'd end up in prison, yet your belief in me never faltered. Even when my 'Carry On' film obsession resulted in me pinching every bottom in sight, you refused to accept the 'sexually inappropriate' label that was attached to me. You knew I was just copying what I had seen on TV and trying to get a reaction. You were firm with me, and disciplined me, but you also tried to understand my behaviour too, because the best way of solving a behavioural issue is to find out the cause. You saw the person beneath the challenging behaviour and you encouraged him, supported him and more than anything you loved him.

And although I've always loved you deeply, I guess I haven't always been great at showing it. In my younger years I was prone to violent outbursts and it still shames me to admit that I punched you in the face twice. I'll always regret that. And do you know what? You were never bitter about it. You never bore a grudge. There must have been times when I seemed so ungrateful, uncooperative and unpleasant and yet you kept going. I guess that's the biggest lesson I've learned from you in life, Mum, to never give up. To see the goal and keep going for it until you achieve it.

I know that you struggled to tell me about my diagnosis. You weren't sure when would be the right time to tell me about having Asperger's, and I can understand that totally. As a child who never wanted to be perceived as different, you knew it would be earth shattering for me to find out that I had a disability. In hindsight I wish you'd told me straight away, but I fully understand why you didn't. What matters most to me is that you never portrayed Asperger's in a negative way. You were always totally positive about my diagnosis and never allowed me to see it as a set back. And that's no mean feat when I'm sure you were worried about my future at times yourself.

Despite six suspensions from school, changing schools and depressive bouts in my early teens, somehow we got there, didn't we? With the support of a great team at my secondary school and a fantastic music therapist, we turned it all around and I got ten

A*–Cs at GCSEs and three A–Cs at A Level. I say 'we', because although I did the work in the classroom, it was only due to you fighting for me that I was allowed into one in the first place!

I now have a good circle of friends, a great relationship and a career. I've toured the country as a speaker and have been published in four countries as a journalist. Not bad for 22, eh? And not bad for a child who was proclaimed a monster. It feels like an even bigger achievement because, in my heart of hearts, I know that if it hadn't been for your love and determination, things would have been very different.

You indulged my many obsessions (even though I'm sure they bored you to tears at times! Who wants to hear about *EastEnders* ad nauseam for 12 months?), you encouraged my sense of humour and most of all you were one of the only people who focused on what I could do rather than what I couldn't. Most importantly you never referred to me as your 'autistic child'. When my diagnosis came, you didn't treat me any differently, because you saw me as a person. Your son, Dean.

I get comments all the time from my peers about my relationship with you. They can't believe how open I am with you. But to me that's a great compliment, because I feel that our mother–son bond has matured into a strong friendship as I've grown into adulthood. Who'd have thought it?

So when I'm asked, at those conferences, whether you're proud of me, I always say the same thing: 'I hope that she is, because I'm totally proud of her.' I love you, Mum.

Dean xxx

About Dean

Dean Beadle tours the UK giving keynote, motivational and after-dinner speeches at conferences, meetings and training events. Having spoken everywhere from Lincoln and Liverpool to Essex and Edinburgh, and most places in between, he speaks about his experiences with Asperger's syndrome; discussing how he developed from a child considered a 'monster' to an A-Grade student. Dean encourages his audiences to see the condition in a much more positive light, through his humorous and poignant anecdotes. In 2011 Dean's speaking brought him to a global audience, as a clip of one of his speeches has been viewed in 75 countries worldwide on YouTube.

Aside from speaking work, Dean is an experienced journalist. He has written articles based on autism for *Cerebra Bulletin* and *NAS Communication Magazine*. He also resided as an online columnist for special needs website www.snapchildcare.co.uk for 18 months. Between 2008 and 2010, Dean was a columnist for commercially released magazine *Autism File*, which was sold in retail chains across the UK, Australia, Dubai and North America. He has also written general news articles and features for www.newsshopper.co.uk and *the londonpaper*. Throughout 2009 he had an economising column in *Greenwich Time* newspaper called 'MR BUDG£T' and between January and May 2010 he had a diet and fitness column in the same publication entitled 'Lighten Up!' Dean has also written book/music/live reviews for the publication.

Most recently he has branched out into presenting work, having presented an online resource for TwoFour Media/The Teaching Development Agency.

B. Hannah's thoughts

It does not matter how positively a parent may try to explain the autism to their child, it is still impossibly easy for them to take it the wrong way. The very concept itself is a negative one, so, although it is up to the parent whether or not they would want to tell their young child now or later, keep in mind that it might not have a particularly warm reception. Even if the negativity wears off quickly, the person affected probably won't have a full picture of their condition, as they have lived with it all their lives. When I'm asked, 'How does it feel to be autistic?' my reply is, 'How does it feel to be neurotypical?'

With regards to the label, I only see it positively in a legal sense, such as getting an individualised programme that would otherwise be inaccessible. Otherwise, I'm neutral, almost negative about the label. As a wannabe author/screenwriter, I don't want people judging my work by my condition – there is a massive difference between 'Wow, this is brilliant' and 'Wow, this is brilliant for an autistic teenager'.

One reason why I admire my family is because, from what I gather, they broke the stereotype of a parent breaking down into tears at the thought that their child required special education. Rather, they realised something was wrong (I knew I should've pointed to my nose on that day!), and they accepted the diagnosis with good grace.

Having said that, they're all barking mad anyway!

A friend of my grandmother's came round one day for a visit, and in my echolalic way, I told her about how I'll never be independent. She then asked me a question that has drastically altered my thinking since – 'How would you define independence?'

It's true, though. One big issue for parents is their concern that someone with autism would not be able to look after themselves as their peers would be able to.

One of the triads of autism is a lack of imagination. I know I'm not one to talk, but please do not take it literally. While there are only about 100 savants in the world (of which only half are autistic), the overwhelming majority are specialist in the creative arts, and the few that aren't are into technology. This certainly does not mean that everyone with the diagnosis is Rainman, but it does mean that most of us do have creative imagination. Just as a heads-up, the definition of imagination is limited to social imagination, such as what would happen if one would order a pizza at a restaurant instead of a burger. I believe my best personal trait is my ability to prioritise. At the moment, I'm aspiring to be a screenwriter – a creative task if ever there was one. The stories I want to write, both in prose and in script, literally take over my life, as I'm sure is the case with most authors. However, the autism highlights the stories to the extent that I cannot think of anything else. For instance, I am writing these points down in a hotel near Chester (I'm actually from Surrey), and tomorrow I'm going to be diving with sharks in an aquarium, because one of the characters in my stories is a blacktip reef shark.

About Hannah

Hannah was born in 1994 and diagnosed with classic ASD three years later. After spending four years in a school for students with moderate learning difficulties, and four years at another school dedicated to autism, by the age of 12, she became home-educated through an individual package due to difficulties at school. Her main interests are animals – especially dinosaurs and aquatic life – and her stated goal in life is to become an author and/or screenwriter.

C. Alex's letter

Dear family,

I give thanks to God for putting me in a Christian family. God has helped me more than anything else – I believe God has helped me through my family and the therapy I have received. I also belong to the Church family. I think Church has helped me to socialise because there are people I have grown up with who just accept me.

As you know, when I was younger I found the world to be a terrifying place. Even something as simple as going into a shop for me was torture. But you have all helped me to understand better that there is little to be afraid of in a shop. You have got me to go into shops and taught me that the world isn't actually that scary. You helped me to overcome some of my fears by slowly introducing me – I know I had a pushchair until I was seven because I was so afraid of the shops. Mum, you used a schedule with pictures to help me get through the day.

I used not to be able to talk very well – I spoke in my own language but I thought I was talking just like everybody else. I remember getting very angry. I didn't understand why no one understood me. Mum, I remember a special box with lots of cards with words and fun things. You worked with me every day and helped me to speak. After this I still stammered – again this would make me get very angry. But this was also improved a few years later when I had therapy and you taught me to stop and think before I spoke. I remember also being taught to say, 'I can't find the word.'

I used to need to flap and clap my hands all the time. This is something I do to help me think about the past and all the things that have gone on during the day. I also do it when I am excited or am thinking about a subject I am obsessed with. I have always enjoyed doing this, although now I like to play with a thread. The first person who tried to stop me doing this was my teacher at the special school I attended for a few years. I hated being told to have good hands. When I started ABA therapy at home I was encouraged not to do this during therapy sessions. I didn't like this but am now glad that this was done. I don't believe stimming should be stopped altogether, but there are times when it is best to control it. I can see how it would stop me from taking in the things people were teaching me. It also looks odd and people can think you are having a fit or may bully you. I remember a few years ago (August 2009) I was staying in a caravan with you all. There was no private space for me to stim so I decided to go behind the caravan. There I was really going for it. What I didn't realise was the man in the next caravan could see me – he came up to me and asked if I was all right. I said I was and he asked if I was sure – I said yes. He then went and found my mum and told her he was worried I had had a fit. Even though I didn't like it at the time you have helped me to control it in social settings. I remember being taught to go to the bathroom if I couldn't control it in a social setting. I still do that now. But thank you for always allowing me time to stim as well.

To the Source (Dad), I am sorry for the times when I didn't like you and wouldn't take hugs from you but would from Mum. I don't hug anyone now. You taught me about history and cameras. I am sorry to say that I liked it when you had a stroke. It made me feel there was someone else in the family who had learning problems and who also needed therapy. I found it hard when you started to get better and could quickly do things better than me. I know you still struggle with things.

To Nanny in Flint, you have always been a good person to stay with. I have stayed with you when there has been a lot going on at home and I have enjoyed the peace and quiet. Thank you for always letting me when you can. Granddad was also equally welcoming. I always enjoyed talking to you and all the food you cooked me like sausages and bacon, and you always made sure I had plenty. You didn't always understand my autism but still accepted me as I was. I used to love going for walks with Granddad and Meg the dog and he would read me stories.

To the W (Mum), you cook some very nice dinners and I very much appreciate that. As I have said earlier you have helped me in many areas. If it wasn't for all your help I wouldn't be where I am today. Even now you are the one who helps me with my talks and even this letter. You come up with ideas for me to improve. I then work on these things with Donna who has worked with me since I was eight.

John, I know you are my big brother. I remember I used to refuse to go to bed unless you were with me.

I must have been hard work for you, and I am sorry you had so much to cope with. I also remember all the games you and Jane used to play with me like shopping, and an evil villain called Scudder. Thank you for all of that – it was fun. I remember you telling me off – I guess that's what big brothers do, though. I didn't like it, even though I always looked up to you and wanted to be like you. You always wanted me to play football with you and to watch the football with you. I know you found it hard not having a 'normal' brother.

Jane, big sister. I am sorry for all those years that I hated you and wouldn't even take a drink from you. I don't really understand why I was like that. I was like that with Dad as well. I really liked it when you and John used to play games with me like Scudder. I really enjoyed those games! I also quite liked it when you helped me with my photography course. I like playing some of the games you have brought back from Beach Mission like Mafia and Psychiatrist.

To my two younger sisters, Ruth and Rebecker. You were the two people in my family I remember as babies. I really liked it when you were newborn babies – I thought you were both really cute. You used to always make me play games with you. I liked the way you both joined in with my therapy before you were two. I liked to think the therapy was for you as well as me. I remember finding it hard when you could do things I couldn't. I always felt that if I was older I should be able to do more than you. I have never liked it when you won't always let me explain my point of view on something. I know I have upset you sometimes and I don't understand why or how I have. I know I have gained so much from having you both around – I am so glad that God gave me two more sisters. You have helped me in more ways than I can count.

Sooty the dog, I love you because you are so cute. But at the same time you can be annoying. I sometimes get tired of taking you for walks, you sometimes bark when I'm on the computer, but I like stroking you and playing with you. You accept me for who I am – there are times when I annoy others but you don't get annoyed. You do bark at me if I get upset, though, but I think this is because you are worried. I know taking you for walks has given me a little independence and responsibility. I sometimes can't read your body language, but I am learning. Thank you for being there for me – I know it can't have been easy. I don't know where I'd be today without you. I think the hard work has made me happier than I would have been without it.

Alex Lowery

About Alex

Alex was 18 years old at the time of writing this letter. He does a lot of public speeches about autism to different organisations. He is quite interested in photography and takes photos of all sorts of things. He mostly likes taking photos of landscapes, seascapes and nature. He is also pretty interested in film making although he hasn't made a film in a while. He finds it difficult to decide what the most important things in his life have been – the day when he said his first words was important; the day his behaviour started to improve, thanks to therapy; and when he was first asked to do a public speech. As for plans for the future, Alex hopes to continue with his photography and maybe do public speaking for a job. But he really doesn't know what he'll be doing for sure. The two biggest hopes in his life are extremely simple and things that most adults take for granted. Those two things are work and independence. He really hopes desperately that he can achieve that. He has a life coach who is working with him to improve his life skills, so there is hope. 'I'll achieve a lot.'

Section comments

These letters and thoughts are included with the absolute minimum of editing – minor typos and layout. The words have not been tampered with. When I asked Dean, Hannah and Alex for their contributions I was not sure what to expect; but what I received left me very affected. The contributions are for me moving, uplifting, painful, insightful, clever...so many different things. But what they attest to is the absolute centrality of your family to your achievements, well being and future prospects. It would not always have felt that way, to the child or the parents. These three families went through some very rough patches. But in the end it is crystal clear how vital the role of parents is and how much they mean to their children at so many different levels. That is a message that I hope all the parents who read this book will take away.

Dear all

Considering some general topics and decisions that come up in the parenting process

This section contains prose pieces addressed to all families. These are some of the broader topics that have come up frequently in my work with families and are general issues that many families will need to consider. They are in some ways independent of specific family circumstances.

A. The road ahead: Looking at how the parenting agenda changes over time

This first piece is addressed to parents who are in the early stages of working out what to do now that they know that their child is differently abled and that it is a long-term issue. The child may be newborn or several years old depending upon the nature of the challenges and the ease or accessibility of diagnosis.

Dear all,

Over time professionals have viewed parents of children with developmental disabilities in a range of quite different ways. Sometimes parents have been blamed for the disabilities themselves and are still often blamed for their child's behaviour. Sometimes the parents have been viewed as emotionally damaged by the experience and as irrational in their demands. A common view like this of recent decades was to view the experience and functioning of parents in a quite uniform way as based on emotional reactions that pass through a series of set stages (based on a model of 'bereavement'). Irrespective of who the parents were, their life circumstances and the nature of the child's challenges, all went through denial, anger, rejection, guilt, resignation and on to acceptance when the parents have finally 'come to terms' with their child's 'disability'. The subtext of this view was that until parents reached that final stage of 'coming to terms' with their situation they were not really rational and their opinions were driven by the emotion dominating the stage they were at. This had the effect of downgrading the significance of parental opinion and demands, as these were seen more as symptoms of emotional distress rather than as a valid and important point of view deserving of respectful attention. Indeed it was even suggested that offering practical help was positively counterproductive until the parents had 'come to terms'.

Although this way of thinking was helpful in drawing attention to the great emotional challenges of bringing up a child with significant long-term difficulties, it effectively discounted the equally great practical challenges and the need for practical supports. It also overlooked the vast number of contributors to parental functioning and the very wide range of individual differences between both the children and their families. The reactions of parents will depend upon who they are as individuals, the quality of the relationship between them, the specific nature of the child's difficulties, the age and stage of the child and other family members, and the quality of support services received...to name but a few factors! The reality is that rather than moving through a series of staging posts en route to the promised land of 'acceptance' there is a long and winding road with many twists and turns, some periods of going round in circles and no clear journey's end. Emotions of all kinds will continue to be evoked. The key proposition is that parents will know and understand their own child a lot better than anyone else and have a more informed view of his or her needs. The opinions of parents therefore become of central importance rather than some peripheral symptom of their distress. Many professionals would now accept these propositions, at least in their verbal behaviour!

So, much has changed over the years. We have moved on to a more positive view of parents and a better understanding of family needs. We have shed earlier rigid views, but there are certainly things that all families face and stages in life where different issues come to prominence, and it may be helpful to consider some of these.

What you will find yourself doing

In the early years, particularly if your child is diagnosed in the first few years of life, you will be very preoccupied with doing hands-on things with your child – following programmes of action that you hope will maximise your child's development. You will be searching for and developing your view about the practical interventions that most benefit your son or daughter. Some parents will pick and choose from a range of options, others will focus on and become adherents of one particular approach (ABA, Options, Floor Time, Portage, Conductive Education...the list of specific 'schools of thought' is very long indeed). Some of you will have help from services in this quest and in delivering the interventions, some not.

As your child gets older and goes to school full time you will find your focus gradually shifting to monitoring the services that you receive, seeking new services, advocating and championing your child and sometimes going to war with service-providing agencies to get the supports that you believe your child needs... and that he or she is not receiving. You will meet professionals who will respond positively, agree with you and work with you; but you will find also that you will need to challenge doctors, teachers, social workers and bureaucrats of all sorts to get what you want. You will learn to do that and you will succeed quite often as long you are very persistent (see 'Managing the system'). You might think that there are professionals paid to assess your child's needs, search out the very best services available, offer them to you and monitor how things progress. You might think that you have enough on your plate getting through day-to-day life. These are not unreasonable thoughts. But the reality is that each child is a unique individual and you do understand things about your child that no one else does and if you do not stand up assertively the system will not respond. The 'system' itself has many flaws including lack of appropriate training for some staff, variability in personal commitment, poor coordination between or within agencies (does the left hand ever know what the right hand is doing?!), significant staff turnover and, of course, resource limitations. It is the family that carries the story and provides the bedrock consistency and deep personal knowledge that is needed to drive forward and sustain the supports that the child/young person/adult needs. You will learn that if you do stand up and persist you will often (not always) get the things that people told you previously you could not have. Hell hath no fury like a parent spurned!

As your son or daughter moves towards adulthood your thoughts turn more and more to planning for the future, including a future when you are not around.

What you will find yourself thinking about

Especially in the early years but probably throughout your life you will be focused for much of the time on matters of immediate concern – managing life day-to-day, getting the services you need now. You will need to make sure that you devote this energy to all your children, not just to the one tagged 'special'. The special one will take up more of your time, but remember doing the right thing by your children is giving quality consideration to issues not necessarily spending exactly the same time on them for all the children (see 'Brothers and sisters').

Every so often (and with increasing frequency as you and your child grow older) you will lift your eyes to the far horizon and think about the longer term – what will your child do as an adult, who will look after him or her, how will he or she be cared for especially once you are gone or differently abled yourself? Then the panic sets in; you have no clue how this will be managed. And then there are the regular horror stories about cruelty, neglect and incompetence meted out to adults with long-term developmental difficulties. The future is a nightmare and many parents will have thoughts that they would prefer their child to die before they do. These are thoughts that no other parent has, and this in turn brings with it additional discomfort in terms of guilt or despair. You quickly learn to shut out long-term thinking and go back to the day-to-day. Day-to-day may be hard but it is more controllable. However, you will return regularly to thinking about the future (despite your best efforts!) and we need to say a few things about how to manage this thinking so that it is not dominated by nightmare scenarios and hopelessness.

Wrestling with a future uncertain

I started my career 40 years ago, working in a long-stay hospital for the 'mentally handicapped' where we had 'wards' full of children and adults with all kinds of developmental disabilities. These people had little stimulation, with most having no organised daytime activities; the children were only just being allowed to go to school. Many 'patients' did not have their own clothes but were dressed from a communal store; they ate food sent out from the central kitchen and slept in dormitories containing up to 70 people with no privacy of any kind. It was a nightmare, a nightmare that has now ended thanks to improvements in our understanding, improvements in the services available and the fact that parents now keep their children at home and bring them up themselves. It was always my understanding that there was an implicit social contract in this policy shift ('community care') – that if parents brought up their children we would provide services that would support this and we would provide services of guaranteed quality, unlike the institutional services provided in the past. I looked forward to the day when we could honestly say to parents: 'You can trust us…when you are gone or unable to cope any more we will provide services that guarantee your son or daughter will be respected, treated kindly and lead a fulfilling life.' That day never came.

But the fact that you cannot relax and rely on quality services when you are not around does not mean that the future is bleak. Far from it. It does mean that there are risks, and so our thinking about the future needs to have an element of risk management. There may be uncertainties, but in reality all life is like that – there are very few things that can be relied upon 100 per cent and we manage to live our lives with these uncertainties. So when you are thinking about the future and doomsday scenarios are starting to dominate, here are a few things to help manage these thoughts constructively and avoid the downward spiral to despair:

- Over the last 40 years we have seen a steady increase in the quantity, quality and diversity of services available. That trend will continue. Yes, there will be shortfalls and quality failures, but these will continue to reduce.

- Particularly important is the new trend towards person-centred planning so that instead of trying to fit someone into a placement, we think about what life will work for someone and build the services and supports around the individual to achieve that life. The trend towards personalisation will continue and offers hope for a better deal for your unique family member.

- Although the trend is away from congregating people with similar labels together in services and to go for more individualisation, there remain many congregate services. The market will remain diversified as some families will prefer group homes, village communities and the like. Because the fashion/ideology is changing does not mean that all services in the future will involve people living on their own in flats and working in supermarkets. The reality is of an ever more diversified range of services.

- A major challenge for us is service accountability. Quality failures occur and are sometimes only discovered when somebody blows the whistle and/or there is an investigative report by TV or newsprint journalists. Such scandals are a recurring feature of our service provision; they are every parent's worst nightmare and a matter of shame for us as a society. However, the trend toward learning how to make services accountable, learning how to monitor quality and avoiding these kinds of catastrophic failures is an upward one. We have a number of systems available for helping services raise and maintain their standards and a number of systems for monitoring quality. They are not perfect by any means, but they are better than what we had before. Again, we can expect that trend to continue.

So although it is reasonable to worry about the future, panic is not necessary and disaster scenarios should not predominate. For every terrible story of abuse and neglect there are ten fabulous stories of great things happening – lives moving on in positive and constructive ways. The question is how best to manage the risks. Here are a few thoughts:

- Start early – start thinking about the kind of future you think would work for your son or daughter from early adolescence. Do not wait for the markers the system has in place (14 or 16) – start thinking as early as feels right for you as a family.

- Organise your thinking in a holistic way – about the overall lifestyle that would suit your child rather than just in terms of specifics ('he needs a job', 'she should go to college'). Learn as much as you can about person-centred planning as that will give you tools to think in this kind of way. Then you will be ready to respond to a system that tends to think in terms of 'placements' – which placement will your son or daughter go to? Your child needs a life not a placement. If you have a clear idea of what you want, it makes it easier to be specific in what you advocate for. This increases the likelihood that you will get what you want and reduces your dependence on having to choose from the menu that service-providing agencies say is available.

- Think about the 'active protection' elements you can put in place for your child for when you are no longer able to keep an eye on things. We need someone/some people who will maintain oversight on how things are going for your child and who will be prepared to step in if things are not going right. The individuals who do this are most likely to come from within the family circle – brothers/sisters, cousins, aunts/uncles. There is a trend towards independent advocacy services and some families may want to go down a route of involving someone who will operate in this way on a more 'professional' basis. It would be better if this kind of protective element involved more than one person, but family circumstances will dictate what is realistic.

Uncertainty cannot be avoided. But it can be reduced and risks can be managed. It means facing the issues head on and preparing rather than avoiding. Avoidance will not only leave you vulnerable to having to take just what is offered to you by the system but also leaves you particularly vulnerable to unpredicted, catastrophic life events. If there is no overall view in place about your child's future needs then decisions in a crisis will be driven by expediency rather than by your son or daughter's best interests.

And a thought for yourselves

As always, the focus of all these words has been on your special child. Bringing up your child is a huge physical and mental challenge. It can burn you out as an individual and it puts a tremendous strain on a relationship if you have a partner. If you are going to do the best job, you have to take care of yourself and any relationship that you are in. This does not mean that you have to party every night or go to the gym every day. It does mean that you need to look at your life and find spaces that are just for you as an individual or as a couple. It may not be frequent, it may not be regular, but those spaces need to be there. I remember talking with a couple who were bringing up three children, one of whom had special needs. As in many couples the way things were divided up meant that the mother did most of the activities with the child with special needs, the father did likewise with the other children. I remember them saying: 'We have a worry that if we keep on like this we will look at each other in ten years' time and realise that we no longer know each other.' Don't let that happen to you.

B. Who are you? Reflecting on how to see real people in the midst of significant and widespread differences in abilities and the diagnostic labels that often accompany these differences

This second piece looks at the challenges of seeing real people in the midst of significant and widespread differences in abilities.

Dear all,

Many of your children have prominent 'technical' labels attached to them – autism, Asperger's syndrome, tuberous sclerosis, Down's syndrome, fragile X, attention deficit hyperactivity disorder, Williams syndrome...to name but a few. They may have more than one of these labels. They may have acquired these labels before birth, at birth, in the first few years of life or after several years of life. These labels are a mixed blessing, and before we examine some of the difficulties we will look at some of the very important and positive functions that they serve (because this is not a rant against 'diagnosis').

The diagnostic labels that we use currently have evolved a lot in the last 50 years or so. Now they may point to some common underlying problems that might not be immediately obvious. Over the years, as our understanding has grown around these labels, it has helped us to construct helpful supports and interventions tailored to the specific needs of children so identified, be it movement skills interventions for children with Down's syndrome or communication skills programmes for children with autism. Such developments have been facilitated because research has been organised around these specific diagnoses and this research has been much more useful than research around more global identifiers such as 'mental handicap/mental retardation'. So this way of categorising people has assisted research and the development of tailored interventions. The diagnoses help parents understand more precisely what is going on for their child and point them in the direction of information that might be specifically helpful for their individual child. They help to connect parents to other parents who may be experiencing similar difficulties, thus reducing that sense of isolation that so many parents experience. You know you are not alone in what you are dealing with and that there are others also facing these issues. This offers parents potentially an important source of social support, especially as many of these diagnoses now have specific national and international parent-led organisations developed around the label. Relief, support, practical help – all these benefits have developed around diagnosis.

Research and support also now start to come together in powerful ways. Many of the parent organisations run websites, courses, publications and conferences, some involving access to highly specialised consultants, to ensure that up-to-date knowledge is readily available to families. This has practical benefits and more generally empowers parents in their battles to get the services and supports that their child needs. These organisations often raise money to fund research that is of the most immediate relevance for families, thus influencing the 'research agenda'. Without this funding stream, research is more likely to be driven by the interests and needs of the academics, their employing institutions and traditional funding bodies, which are not necessarily the same as the interests and needs of families.

Finally, specific diagnosis is becoming increasingly important as a 'ticket' for accessing relevant services and supports. Services are becoming increasingly organised around specific diagnostic labels so that you cannot access the service without the diagnosis. Whether this is a good or bad thing is neither here nor there – it is the reality for many parents and this means that a diagnosis is very important to them.

So there are many benefits linked to an accurate diagnosis based upon the categorisation systems that we use currently (which do change – the diagnoses and their criteria are regularly updated, usually by an agreement reached among the high-status professionals who review these matters). But there are downsides which need to be understood so that they can be counteracted. I will draw attention to three related issues:

- *Overshadowing.* These labels are very powerful; they come to define the person almost entirely. You become known by others as 'the child with Down's syndrome/autism' and this is often the first thing people know about you when they first meet you. Nobody identifies me as the left-handed guy with eczema. My CV makes no mention of these factors nor will they appear on the jacket of this book.

- *Negative bias.* All these labels draw attention to things that the individual is not good at or cannot do. They stress 'abnormality'. Anne Fortis, a public speaker with Down's syndrome, used to say that she thought it should have been called Up syndrome as that is how she felt about it and how she would like others to think about it. I will often be introduced as an author and presenter (areas of strength for me) not as the guy who cannot fix anything and has next to no useful practical skills (unless my wife has been having a particularly frustrating time with my incompetence and vents this in company!). So looked at from the point of view of the individual, he or she is defined by powerful labels with strong connotations of inability and incompetence. Individuals are even said to 'suffer' from these labels (autism, fragile X, etc., etc.). This is not something that the rest of us would aspire to (I have never thought of myself as 'suffering' from left-handedness, or sinistralism, as we should probably call it). It is not about denying difficulties – there is an equal and opposite madness of the happy, clappy, we can only say positive things type. What is needed is a clear and balanced view of who the person is as a whole – strengths and weaknesses – rather than a one-sided view, which links to the next point...

- *Atomisation.* Part of the overshadowing process is that right away the individual is seen in terms of one or two specifics. He or she is not really seen as a whole person. The person is reduced to a small number of negatively viewed parts. Indeed much of his or her subsequent life will be taken up with attention to a small number of specifics with which he or she struggles to be competent (special education rather than education). This process is often mirrored in how services are organised, with a large number of professionals involved, each dealing with one small part of the picture, no one having an overview. This makes it hard to see the real person and the real life that we are dealing with.

These issues are not just philosophical or theoretical. They lead to a number of practical consequences. First, as already stated, it becomes hard for people to relate to the individual as a real, whole person. Being seen in a fragmented way with differences and difficulties emphasised may encourage the idea that the individual is not fully human or is some kind of alien and therefore, perhaps, does not have to be treated in the same way as others. This kind of dehumanisation has been clearly implicated in many of the disastrous quality failures in services that have resulted in the abuse of those using the services. But more than that, growing up around attitudes that do not see you as a fully formed human being, even if the individual is not specifically abused, can have long-term psychological consequences. It is hard to grow up feeling good about yourself if others do not feel good about you.

The negative bias means that the emphasis of interactions in life is very much on what the individual cannot do or finds difficult. He or she spends a lot of time working on areas of difficulty or incompetence. Imagine growing up spending all your time working on the things that were a real challenge to you, being reminded for a very large part of every day about what you do not get or only get with great difficulty. Imagine the focus of every discussion about you being the things that you cannot do. It would be hard to grow up feeling good about yourself if your everyday experience was like this.

The atomisation means that there may be whole areas of the person that are never recognised – personality, life story, quirks, passions and eccentricities, the rituals to which the individual attaches great importance, how his or her mind works, the things that grab his or her attention and engage his or her motivation, the little signals he or she gives off and what they mean. All this kind of real human information is either not acknowledged or relegated to the background while we foreground the 'disabilities'. It would be hard growing up feeling good about yourself if these aspects of you were not acknowledged and celebrated.

So this piece is about a number of things. It is about how we get to know the people we are thinking about, how we develop insightful, respectful and celebratory relationships so that the children can grow up feeling good about themselves because others feel good about them. But it is about more than that. It is about the personal futures that people access. For all of us, when we are growing up we have to work on things that we enjoy and/or find easy and things that we dislike and/or find hard. But as we move towards our adult lives we start to construct those lives around our strengths and look at how we can avoid or compensate for our weaknesses. We may still have to persevere with things that are difficult for us and we have to be open to taking on new challenges, but the balance most definitely shifts towards the amplification of strengths and the concealment of weaknesses. That is how we find lives that work for us. If life is to work for people with 'disabilities' it has to reflect that very human tendency and not persist with life as a 'broad and balanced curriculum'.

Apart from a lot of high-sounding words and fuzzy sentiments, does all this have any practical implications? It reinforces points made elsewhere – parents must have the confidence that they know their child best, far better than any specialist who knows one small part of their child. It releases parents to do all the things that they would do with any other child, to mess about, have fun, get involved in the child's world so that you deepen your understanding of who your child is and how he or she works. It argues against spending every waking minute 'doing programmes' to remedy your child's prioritised deficits. Of course remedial intervention programmes are important, but keep them in perspective and understand that there are other things that are just as important. Finding areas of mutual pleasure and enjoyment are precious spaces.

These ideas also mean that those who are professionally involved need to take much greater care to gather information that will help build a real understanding of who the child is and how he or she works rather than focusing exclusively on 'symptom checklists' and 'deficit remedying targets'. A lot of these ideas will be found in what is now called person-centred planning, but be careful – the core issue is not which is the right checklist to use but how we foreground the real person here and background the overshadowing labels and biases.

Finally, if we can develop these ideas, if we can communicate them to all those involved and to broader society, if we can get others to see that the labelled ones are just people like us, trying to get by and get a life, then we go a long way towards protecting people from the abusive experiences that have befallen them before...and continue to befall them.

Postscript

Although this letter makes rather light of the checklist culture that pervades so many human services, the fact of the matter is that your diagnosed child will be assessed many times over. Assessment means gathering information, some of which will be done by asking questions. Here are a few questions (not a comprehensive list...and certainly not a checklist!) that can help orient 'assessors' to the real person they are assessing so that it is easier to locate the difficulties in a broader, person-centred context:

- Words to describe the individual
- Who in the family most like
- Personality
- What like if not autistic/Klinefelter's/Williams, etc.
- Things people like and admire
- Important personal likes and dislikes
- Learning style
- Attention preferences – things readily noticed, things not
- Positive rituals...those things that help make the day/life go well
- Best days...worst days (plus 'power' exercise – how to create perfect day, disastrous day)

- What is important TO the person?...including non-negotiables, things that just have to be part of everyday life if it is to be satisfactory
- What is important FOR the person? (Not the same as what is important TO...but also important)
- What have we learned about you...supports that work/don't work
- What do we accept about you?
- What will we seek to change?

Maybe these questions can help guide you as parents to produce a pen picture of your son or daughter to hand over to the next checklist wunderkind who enters the house!

A mother's reflections

Having written the above piece I subsequently received an email from Rudy's mother (see Section 3). We have communicated over many years and I have always felt privileged to learn from the extraordinary insights that she has into Rudy's world view and the ways that she has been able to communicate with him over the years. Rudy has a very unusual take on the world and has 'very complex needs'. However, this is what his mother says, reflecting on their journey together (Rudy is now a young adult):

For me Rudy has always clearly had his differences but at the same time he has always had needs/wants/ similarities in common with the rest of us. In other words I have always looked at what any human being would expect/want to be treated like in a specific situation – taking into account their age, stage of development, values, personality, resources and so forth and adapted and applied that to Rudy – rather than regarding him as an alien species. Sometimes I think the analogy people with Asperger's use about being an alien from Mars can be just as damaging as it can be illuminating for the uneducated in autism. And in many ways I have found that what will work for you and I as non-autistic will also be appropriate and applicable to him – if that makes sense, it just needs adapting perhaps. So stuff like sowing a seed would work for me or for Rudy equally well for instance despite our differences, and I would use that for my other non-autistic son/daughter if I had one. Or I might be persuaded to walk five miles for something I want and value like a ticket to Tom Jones if that was the only way to get one, but Rudy would do the same walk with me for two special coffee sachets because they hold a special significance to him – same process just an adaptation to his differences/what he values/gets him motivated. What I'm trying to say I guess is that autistic people have their differences but also similarities – there is no need to endlessly re-invent the wheel as we know it for autistic people – you may disagree. So for instance I have always given Rudy an explanation I have just adapted it to his needs, age, understanding, framework of reference and so forth – the point being from my perspective he is just as entitled to it as you or I might be. Human rights and all that.

C. Brothers and sisters: Considering the impact on siblings of growing up with a brother or sister who has significant developmental disabilities

This third piece considers the impact on siblings of growing up with a brother or sister who has significant developmental disabilities.

Dear all…or rather, dear all of you who have other children,

Many of you might be concerned about the impact on children growing up with a brother or sister who has significant developmental disabilities. Will the other children be harmed or lose out in some way? Will they grow up disturbed and dysfunctional because of this experience? As with many things, these questions cannot be answered by simple generalisations that apply to all. Families who have a child/children with developmental disabilities are not some kind of uniform group – what they go through and how they go through it shows enormous variability. The impact on family members is influenced by the individual characteristics of each of those members, by the stage of development in life they are at, by the relationships between each member and every other member, by more general factors such as family dynamics, family style, family atmosphere, by the supports available to the family (formal and informal) and by the family's material circumstances and living conditions. Making any kind of general statement that might be of some help to the varied parents who read this book is therefore very difficult. But there are some points to be made that might be reassuring and some that might offer practical guidance.

About parenting

For children to grow up well they do not have to have all their parents' attention. If there is more than one child each child does not have to have an equal share of the parents' attention. Leave aside the issue of a child having some form of significant disability; in any family parents have things to do other than tend to their children and some children are more needy and demanding than others. Children are only damaged by extreme conditions – extreme neglect and/or physical, sexual or emotional abuse. Human development is pretty resilient in the face of large differences between environments in which children are raised. There is no one right way to be a parent, and children will thrive under widely varying parental practices.

It is very likely that the child with special needs will always absorb a lot more of the parental attention available than any brother or sister without such needs. That is how it usually is. In and of itself that situation will not cause harm. The key thing for parents is to make sure first that they can find some 'mental space' for their other children, that they devote some time to thinking about them, considering where they are up to, what their needs might be. Although this sounds obvious it is a way of pointing to one danger that does exist. If absolutely everything about family life revolves around the child with special needs, if, in a sense, that child is the 'dictator' in the family, then such an extreme imbalance will put a lot of pressure on the other relationships within the family. It will strain the relationship between parents and likewise push out the other children. The same thing would be true if family life was controlled entirely by any other member, child, parent or grandparent. Family life has to have some kind of balance so that everyone is considered if the family and all its members are to flourish. So making sure that there is mental space for the other children is a way of remembering this.

Of course it will also help if this kind of mental space can be represented in the real world, if there can be times when the other children have their own access to their parents, doing things that are right for them. These times may be few and far between. The child with special needs will take the 'lion's share'. But if these times exist and if they occur repeatedly (not necessarily frequently or on a planned, consistent basis) then they become a part of the growing-up experience over time and validate the other children as important individuals. Under these circumstances the available evidence and experience suggests that the general outcome will be positive. The brothers and sisters will not sustain long-term damage despite many short-term upsets; and indeed may gain considerable advantages (see below).

This is not to say that parents will not receive complaints from their children, all their children most likely, that things are 'not fair' and the other children get more than the complainant does. Sadly this is the nature of the developing beast, which is never blessed with gratitude overflowing to the parent(s)!

Being a sibling

There is no doubt that growing up with a brother or sister who has developmental disabilities can bring many challenges. We have already discussed the issue of 'access' to your parents (mental and physical). Your brother or sister can be the source of many disruptions – spoiling your games, damaging your stuff, making it hard to concentrate when homework needs to be done, physically hurting you, being rude to you. He or she can be a source of social embarrassment so that you are reluctant to invite friends home or include your sibling with the outside activities that you do with your friends. As well as these specific, problematic interactions the overall quality of the relationship between siblings may vary. But this is true of all sibling relationships – you may have a fundamentally good relationship...or not: you may not get on at all and there may exist considerable hostility between you.

But alongside the challenges are the gifts. All those of us who have shared lives over extended periods of time with people identified as 'disabled' understand the profound, and I would argue positive, effect that this has upon our views of people in general, the human condition and the societies in which we live. We learn things and gain perspectives that would otherwise have been denied to us. A dimension is added to our thinking. There is also much fun to be had. The view of 'disability' commonly promoted tends to emphasise tragedy, sadness, loss, deficits. The reality also includes laughter, amazement, wonder and bemusement. Families find themselves in the most extraordinary situations, some of which are uproariously funny (once you have overcome the embarrassment bit). Brothers and sisters share in these experiences and also access the sometimes quirky views of the world that their brother or sister can open up for them. Brothers and sisters also gain from the enhanced maturity that comes with this territory. You have to grow up faster and take more responsibility than other young people. Some may regard this as a problem, but it also offers you considerable advantages in a number of real-world situations, such as getting a job or accessing vocational training. This experience may well influence career choice, nudging siblings towards more 'human service' type work. It is of course a matter of opinion whether this is a good or bad thing.

There is also now much more help specifically targeted towards siblings. There are books, support groups (real and virtual), camps and other leisure activities – all things that help to build understanding, reduce isolation, relieve stress and to have some fun (it is hoped!).

So the lived experience of brothers and sisters is a mixed bag, with gains as well as losses. The evidence is that in general brothers and sisters are not damaged by growing up with a sibling who has developmental disabilities. There will be individual exceptions to this but the general, long-term picture is a positive one. There are challenges and stresses but there are gifts and gains as well. As long as the family functions in the interests of all its members and respects and values all its members (is not dominated by one member to the exclusion of all others) then resilience and enrichment in the face of the challenges is what we will see.

After we are gone

Children grow up. Parents grow old. The vast majority of the children with disabilities with whom this book is concerned will need some kind of extra help and support throughout their lives. The question then arises as to the role of the brothers and sisters as the capacities of the parents decline or they die.

Once again there will be tremendous differences between families and also large cultural differences in terms of expectations that are laid upon the siblings. There will also be individual differences in the expectations that siblings are prepared to fulfil. From my point of view I would want to focus on two areas. First, the question of what happens when parents are gone is not one to be decided all at once and would be better decided together rather than by the diktat of one or only some of those involved. These are difficult conversations that need to go on intermittently, preferably over many years. The topic needs to be out in the open and worked on together (parents and their older children) and should be broad based. That means that it is not just about what the brothers or sisters will do but about developing a shared vision of the kind of life that we are working towards for the person identified as disabled; and then what role the brothers or sisters will play in this life. There are likely to be disagreements, which is why time is needed and an early start preferable (not waiting until a crisis falls upon the family) so that these can be worked through and some mutually acceptable resolution found.

The second point should be seen more as a personal plea. From my point of view the thing that is important above all else for the child/adult with developmental disabilities is that the brothers and sisters retain a relationship with him or her and are prepared to advocate vigorously on his or her behalf, whatever else they do. The long-term welfare of those with developmental disabilities is very dependent upon advocacy support and advocacy based upon blood ties and long-term involvement is going to be much more powerful than any kind of 'independent' or service-based advocacy. At the end of the day family provides the most crucial set of relationships for us all. So whatever else goes on in a family, whatever things are 'right' culturally, it is important to avoid the scenario where relationships break down and are severed, thus precluding that vigorous long-term advocacy support that I would regard as critical to the long-term well being of the adult with special needs.

With so many factors that influence the outcomes for a family it is hard to say much that is sensible and of practical help. But I hope that I have been able to provide some broad brush guidelines on how to manage these issues and some reassurance that despite the huge day-to-day challenges that will be dominating your thinking, things generally work out well in the long term, sometimes very well indeed.

D. Managing the system: Thoughts about dealing with the challenges that arise for parents having to deal with multiple professional agencies over long periods of time

This next piece looks at some of the challenges that arise from having to deal with multiple professional agencies over long periods of time.

Dear all,

By the time you come to read this I am sure that you will have found yourselves dealing with a large number of agencies and individuals who are paid to provide services to those with 'special needs'. The agencies may be in the health, education or social service sectors; they may be statutory, voluntary or private. The services will range from assessments of many kinds, advice and consultation through to more direct forms of provision (nurseries, schools, home education, leisure, respite care). Most of the people that you meet will be nice. Some will not be. They will vary enormously in their understanding of and experience with your child's specific issues. All will be constrained in terms of what they can offer you. You will find quite a lot of your time will be taken up in meeting with these people, sometimes on their territory, sometimes in your own home, and a lot of them will want you to fill in forms. Most will believe that they understand your child, that they are personally competent and that they are working in the best interests of your child. This level of professional involvement in your life is a whole new world for most families. Family life becomes, in this sense, 'professionalised'. This can feel quite overwhelming and quite alienating. There is a loss of privacy and a lot of people end up knowing an awful lot of information about some of the most intimate aspects of your family life. There follows a few thoughts about managing this 'system'.

Remember who you are

You are your child's parent. You have the most extensive knowledge of him or her. You spend the most time with him or her and you know better than anyone what makes your child tick – how your child operates, what your child can and cannot do, what your child loves and hates, what works and what does not work. You also have a commitment to him or her like no one else. You may not have all the specialised knowledge that may be linked to your child's 'condition', but you know your child as the real person that he or she is. You will meet professionals who know things that you do not, you will find that they can have interesting perspectives that you had not considered, and you will find that your child, just like every other child, may behave very differently with other people compared to how he or she behaves with you. But when push comes to shove you know best what is right for your child. Certainly listen to others and learn all you can from them, but if what is suggested to you does not feel right then the chances are it is not right. Your child very much depends upon you to stand up for what is right for him or her. So it is important to approach with confidence your engagement with the system and not to be intimidated by 'professionals'. They have an important role to play, but they are there to advise, support and be of assistance. They are not there to take over or direct matters or make decisions on your behalf.

Keep your ear to the ground

From the start of my career there has been the intention to make sure that parents know all the services and entitlements that are available to them. To that end we have tried many forms of 'key workers', endless directories and pamphlets and now, of course, websites. Yet, still today as 40 years ago, many parents find out about useful services through casual conversations with other parents. There is a lesson here. If you want to know what is out there that might be of benefit to your child you need to be an active seeker of information. Talk to other parents, scan the internet, get involved with parent-led organisations dedicated to some of the things that make your child special, question all the professionals you have contact with. In that way you are most likely to be fully up to date with what is going on compared to if you wait for someone to tell you. There will be people whose job it is to coordinate and inform and that will be helpful, but do not rely on them as the sole source of your information.

As well as knowing what is available there is the more difficult issue of knowing about the quality of what is available. How good are the services that are on offer? This is a much more difficult question, partly because the technology of quality control is more difficult and partly because families will vary enormously among themselves in their own standards. That is, families will vary in terms of what they are looking for and what they regard as 'good'. There is some helpful progress being made. We do have regular government inspections of schools, health and social care services, the results of which are publicly available. There may be other forms of accreditation that organisations sign up to (such as the autism accreditation scheme linked to the National Autistic Society in the UK). Most recently attempts are being made to use the 'tripadvisor' model so that people can comment personally on the services that they use with these comments made publicly available. All these sources of information are useful. None of them are foolproof.

One important point to note is that the best-quality evaluative information will come from people who have direct experience of the services and have observed it in action. Evaluation that is based on a service's paperwork is of much more limited value. Glossy brochures, elaborate policy documentation and high-sounding mission statements tell you little about what things are really like. This is an area where saying the right thing is an awful lot easier than doing the right thing. Some services may have great paperwork and terrible practice, some may have terrible paperwork and great practice, and yet others will have both good paperwork and good practice. It is impossible to know this without further research. That means seeing what goes on and communicating with those who actually use a service. These will be your best sources of information about the quality of a service.

Don't be frightened to cause trouble

Parents can be quite overwhelmed by the 'professionalisation' of their lives that occurs once they become engaged with the 'special system'. You will be faced with many 'high-status', sometimes even 'eminent' people. The British in particular can be very reticent about challenging professionals or complaining about the services they receive. But I cannot think of a family I have worked with in the last 40 years that has not learned that you have to fight for what you want. What you want, especially if it falls outside what a service traditionally offers, is rarely given to you just on the basis of the family expressing a preference or highlighting a need. This means conflict with many people that you might traditionally have deferred to. It also means persistence in the face of denial as one argument rarely settles an issue.

Apart from the British 'disease' of suffering in silence there is an additional fear for parents that can inhibit their willingness to stand up to service providers. This is the fear that if I as a parent cause too much trouble then this will be taken out on my child. This is particularly relevant where the conflict is with an agency such as a school or residential service that shares a significant amount of your child's care. Such anxiety is not unreasonable. It would be wrong to imply that such victimisation could never happen. However, I would have to say that is not what I have seen happen in practice. The forcefully assertive parent is much more likely to get the outcome that he or she believes to be in their child's best interest; and the child is not victimised as a result of the confrontation. Staff will certainly moan about the 'pushy' parent, but that will not translate into discrimination against the child…in my experience.

However, there are ways and ways of being 'pushy'. It is rarely productive to get out of control, indulge in personal rudeness or threaten violence. This is much more likely to harden opposition. Much more successful is forceful assertiveness and great persistence – making it clear, quietly and firmly, that you are not going to back down or go away. Over and over again I have seen the sequence of service agencies saying to parents 'No… no…no…no…yes'. Who dares wins!

Hunt in packs…when you can

It is very hard for any family to find the personal resources to sustain the drive to get the services that you believe best serve your child's interests. It is especially hard if you are doing this on your own. You can certainly be made to feel that you are ignorant, unreasonable or selfish in these circumstances. So when it is possible (it is not always possible) work together with other parents to get what it is you all want. Working as a group makes it harder to dismiss the idea as that of one cranky parent and, socially, it is much harder to withstand the pressure that a group can put on compared to the pressure that an individual can put on. Even if you connect to other families who do not have the same needs (for example, in parent groups) the emotional support that you get from others may help to clarify your thinking and give you the energy to persist.

Take care of yourself/ves

Bringing up your child and dealing with service-providing agencies are huge challenges to parents. This is not all downside. There are upsides in terms of what you learn about people and what you learn about yourselves. You discover talents that you never knew you had. But it takes energy and, above all, stamina. There are two areas of advice here. The first is about your mind set. Of course some issues are urgent and have to be dealt with right away. But many are better thought of as marathons rather than sprints. To get your child to achieve what you want, to bring about a change in service provision that you want, will take time and sustained energy. It is about the long haul, dogged persistence and careful management of your energy reserves.

Which takes us to the second point. It is very easy to say 'make sure you take time for yourself' but very hard to do that. Your 'special child' will absorb an enormous amount of your time and emotional energy. You may well have other children and they need your time and energy too. This does not leave you with a lot of space in your life but it is important to think about how energy levels might be sustained. Here are a few thoughts:

- Try to find some support for yourself. You may have a supportive partner…or not; or your partner may be just as exhausted as you. Is there a friend or relative that you could share things with? Are there other parents in a similar position that you could share things with? You do not have to be sharing everything all the time, but you do need someone who can be available to you on a regular basis. It also helps if the sharing itself includes good times as well as difficult times rather than contact only occurring at times of crisis.

- Permit yourself a pampering every so often. Whether it is a long bath, a manicure/pedicure, a haircut, a movie, a tub of your favourite ice cream, time in the garden – whatever it is, award yourself pampering even if it is only once a year. You are entitled to 'treats' so make sure you get them!

- Much more difficult, but try to carve out a part of your life that is not about special needs and disabilityland…and children in general! A job can serve this function but employment can be very difficult to maintain (given the demands on your time both from your child but also from service agencies), certainly for both parents in a two-parent family and even harder for a single parent. Hobbies can serve this function as can additional education. It does not have to be something that you devote a lot of time/effort to. That is likely to be impossible. But just so that there is some part of your life that is about you and not about others.

I am sure that there are many more ideas about keeping our spirits and energy up. But it is not something to be neglected. You cannot be the parent you want to be if you burn out. This is a long haul and you need to be in good shape for something like that.

But remember...

I think that the job of parents of a 'special' child is enormously demanding and it grieves me greatly that I have to say that as well as bringing up your child you will also have to hunt down the services available to you and sometimes do battle with them to get what you want. It has been well understood for a very long time the kinds of pressures that parents are under and the supports that they might need. It is a disgrace that we have not done a better job in developing services that are truly supportive of families. But that is the reality that many families face. On the other side it is also important to remember that we do provide many more services than we did 40 years ago and sometimes the system works really well. You will meet some wonderful people in the system, people who absolutely 'get it', who are knowledgeable, competent and enthusiastic. They will love your child, achieve great things with him or her and understand how it is for you as a family. They will help you understand things and solve the problems that trouble you. It is just that it is not always that way, so it is best to be ready for some of the rougher terrain on the journey.

Postscript...and be a filing clerk too

Your contact with the system will, over the years, generate an awful lot of paperwork. Assessments, service plans, letters, minutes of meetings. There will be a lot of useful information in this paperwork. All agencies will have files on your child and some will have them on you. It would be reasonable to expect that the different agencies communicate effectively with each other. It would be reasonable to expect that different parts of the same agency communicate effectively with each other. It would be reasonable to expect that the agency person sitting opposite you will have read all the information available to him or her on your child. These are all reasonable expectations. They are all likely to be unfulfilled to a significant degree. Interagency communication often breaks down; the left hand regularly fails to know what the right hand is doing and nobody reads much any more. This means that the family has to be right on top of all the information and make sure that those who need to know information get it from you rather than relying on the system. Take it upon yourself to send copies of relevant information to all who you think need it. Take your file(s) with you to meetings. It may also help to write up a 'potted history' of your child to bring up to speed the bright young thing who has recently entered your family life. This in turn means that the family will need to retain copies of all paperwork and develop a good filing system that makes it easy to lay your hands quickly on relevant information. Fair – of course not. Necessary – I'm afraid so.

E. Got behaviour – get drugs? A guide to help parents think through the issues that arise when they are offered medication to help control their son's or daughter's behaviour

This next piece addresses some of the issues for families who are offered medication to help deal with the significant behavioural challenges being presented by their son or daughter.

Dear all...of you considering the use of medication to impact the behaviour of your son or daughter,

Children with developmental disabilities are vulnerable to presenting with significant behavioural difficulties at home and in the community – intense tantrums, physical aggression, self-injury, property damage and a whole host of 'socially embarrassing' behaviours (rude remarks or questions, touching other people, sniffing at other people, spitting, stealing their food...the list is long!). Some of these behaviours do little harm and become tolerable eccentricities. Many of them resolve through good parenting. Some are intense, sustained, dangerous and harder to resolve, putting tremendous pressure on the family as a whole and limiting family life in many, many ways. For these kinds of problems families should be able to access competent, specialised support services. This area of vulnerability has long been known about. Much research has been carried out to develop effective techniques for both assessing these behaviours and for intervening with them so that the individual can move on from dealing with their issues in these destructive ways (behaviours do have a reason and are a way that the individual tries to resolve personally important problems). It should be a no-brainer in the 21st century that parents should have ready, local access to good-quality behavioural support services. Unfortunately the reality can be far from satisfactory and many parents find themselves struggling with very difficult behavioural issues over extended periods of time with little effective support (see Section 3 for vivid illustrations of this reality).

With a family struggling in this way it is quite likely that these concerns will be brought to the attention of the medical services that are involved routinely with the family (either at general practice or consultant level); and at some point the offer will be made to try bringing about behaviour change through the use of medication. At this point it is important to be clear that we are not talking about medications for treating verified medical conditions (for example, antibiotics for infections, anti-convulsants for epileptic seizures). We are talking about medications, euphemistically labelled 'psychotropic', that are offered as a means of changing specific behaviours (such as hallucinations) or changing the emotions that are thought to 'drive' behaviours (such as anxiety or depression). These kinds of drugs divide both professional and lay opinion. People tend to have strong views for or against them as a matter of general principle. The focus of this discussion is not on the general argument. This is not an argument for or against these kinds of medication. It is about the practicalities for families to consider at the point that medication is offered. Nearly all families have a general desire not to use drugs with their children. However, as outlined above, if a family is struggling with very serious behaviours that do not seem to be improving, if no other help is available and the family is essentially going under, then many families will consider medication as a last resort, even if in general they are opposed to using drugs. This discussion is about how families can be helped to make a good-quality decision under these very difficult circumstances.

There are a number of questions that will help to guide the decision-making process. These should be addressed with the professional who is offering to prescribe.

1. *What is the logic of the medication being suggested?* How is the professional viewing the behavioural difficulties, what is he or she seeing that leads to the suggestion of the medication in question as an appropriate intervention for this problem? Does this view seem plausible to you as a parent? Is there any evidence that this particular medication is effective with problems of this kind?

2. *If the medication is potentially effective, what are the specific positive changes that we might expect to see?* It is important to get a clear view of the changes expected – for example, fewer behaviours, behaviours less intense, smiling more, more cooperative with tasks. There are many potential changes and it is important to get as specific as possible about the positive changes that we might expect to see. Once we have this specific list it will greatly help all future drug-related decisions if we set up a system for

monitoring (counting, measuring) these factors. This needs to be as objective as possible and based on changes that we can actually see (specific behaviours) rather than things we have to guess at ('seems better in himself', for example). Measuring these behaviours may involve a chart, a diary, regular videos, rating scales. There are many options here and the professional may have a ready-made system or it may be necessary to make one up to suit the individual circumstances. Most importantly we need to start taking these measures before the drug begins (the baseline) and keep on taking them throughout the time when medication is being used.

3. *What are the known, potential negative side effects of the medication suggested?* For parents to make an informed decision they must know the side effects and their likelihood. This should be discussed with the prescribing professional to make sure that this area is properly understood. Simply being handed a drug company leaflet is not good enough. This will then lead on to a decision about how to monitor whether any of the negative side effects are occurring and what action might be needed if any do occur.

4. *What are the criteria for discontinuing the medication?* From the beginning there should be some idea about how we will decide that the medication has been helpful enough that we can consider discontinuing it. On the other hand it is equally important to know ahead of time what criteria we will use to decide that the medication is playing no significant role and should be removed. The criteria will involve both the size of change that has occurred and its stability (how long it has lasted for). This is important because it is a sad fact that once a person with developmental disabilities is put on psychotropic

medication they often never come off even though no one has any real idea whether it is helpful or not. In that sense everyone becomes dependent upon the medication and is unwilling to take a chance on removing it even though the evidence about its effectiveness is not available. This in turn becomes a self-fulfilling prophecy because the longer you stay on a medication like this the harder it is to withdraw the medication and the more likely there are to be negative side effects such as increases in behaviour if any withdrawal is attempted.

These last points reinforce the importance of objective monitoring (points 2 and 3 above). When the medication is reviewed the monitoring data should always be present and inform the decisions to be made. No decision about continuing, increasing dose, stopping altogether should be made on the basis of 'we think it is/is not helping'. Impressionistic judgement is simply not adequate for competent decision making of this kind.

Making a decision about using medication for behaviour is one of the most difficult and painful decisions that a family has to make. No one wants to drug their child. Yet sometimes this can be a helpful and family-saving intervention. The points raised here will help families make good-quality decisions about the best interests of their son or daughter. It should also be pointed out that both in the UK and USA professional medical bodies have issued very clear guidelines about psychotropic prescribing practices that should be followed by professionals prescribing for people with developmental disabilities. Parents might want to access these. But it is another sad fact that these guidelines have a limited impact on the actual prescribing practices that families may be exposed to.

Finally, there are some statements that parents may find themselves confronted with and for which some preparation may be helpful:

- *Statement 1.* A non-medical service states that they cannot handle your child unless he or she is on medication. This kind of blackmail is completely inappropriate and an indicator of the need to look for another service.

- *Statement 2.* There has been no real change so the prescribing professional suggests an increase in the dose or adding another medication. The need for an increase should not be dismissed, but go through again the criteria discussed in points 1–4 and get clear how far this process goes (is this the maximum dose or are we going to have this discussion again if it is not working? At what point do we decide this drug is not effective, point 4?). More caution is needed about deciding to add another medication. Most practice guidelines advise against multiple medications but do not rule out altogether this possibility. At the very least, adopting this approach requires a quite specific justification rather than being seen as a natural course of action if things are not going well with one drug.

- *Statement 3.* 'He or she is a lot better on the medication and this is because it has corrected biochemical imbalances in the brain, therefore he or she needs to stay on it.' This is pseudoscientific neurobabble. Although we know more than we did about brain functioning we still know very little. It is important to understand that most of the medications called psychotropic were either discovered to have a psychological effect accidentally (they were originally designed for some other purpose) or are derived from these earlier accidental tourists. None are derived from a detailed understanding of the role of brain chemistry in behavioural and emotional functioning. 'Correcting chemical imbalances in the brain' is more medicine show than medical knowledge. However, what can be said is that if someone is on a psychotropic medication for a long time then withdrawal can be very difficult and most services are not set up to manage drug withdrawal. As mentioned above, this is one of the reasons why people can stay on these medications for a very long time, once they have started. This reinforces the need discussed in point 4 about criteria for discontinuation so that we have the best chance of effective help without long-term negative consequences.

As stated many times, the use of medication for behaviour raises strong feelings and 'principled stances'. Yet for many families this moves from being a matter of theory and personal philosophy to a very practical issue as they battle to keep some kind of family life going. It would be a lot better if there were higher-quality behavioural services for families, and the fight for that should continue. However, at any one moment in time a real family in a real situation has to make a tough decision. It is hoped that the discussion here will help such a family make the best possible decision in the circumstances in which they find themselves.

Letters to parents

Thinking about behavioural challenges presented by children and young people on the autistic spectrum

These letters contain the gists of conversations that I have had with a number of families about how to improve the situations that the families find themselves in because of the behaviour of their son or daughter. Some of the families I knew because I was involved as a consultant for some period of time with a service used by their child. Others contacted me directly, usually by email, and I had no involvement in other areas of the child's life. These conversations were conducted face to face, by email, by telephone or any combination of these media. Sometimes the conversations were few in number carried on over a short period of time, sometimes they were many, carried on intermittently over many years.

What these discussions illustrate are the very serious situations that some families find themselves in. Often parents are having to manage these situations with very little relevant professional support. It is hoped that the content of the letters will show how one can think psychologically about the issues and what practical implications follow from the view that we construct about what is going on. I hope also that some readers will pick up useful ideas about ways of improving the difficulties that they are struggling with at home. It is important to stress that these conversations were intended to be of some help but such conversations are no substitute for proper support services. It is a matter of grave concern that even these very articulate families were facing such serious difficulties with so little useful support from local services about how to manage and resolve these difficulties.

All these case studies are real individuals. Details have been changed to reduce the likelihood of identification. The families concerned have given permission for publication in this book.

A. Charlene ('obsessions')

Charlene is a teenager, on the autistic spectrum and with significant generalised learning difficulties. The topic is 'obsessions', which are expressed across all environments (home, school and community) and are increasingly disruptive both to Charlene and to those who share her life. The details about these 'obsessions' are described in the body of the letter.

Dear _____,

Thank you for getting in touch about your daughter Charlene. I was very concerned to hear about how much her life has been taken over by 'obsessions'. This is clearly having a serious impact on family life, making all outings very fraught. It is disrupting her education. The school is struggling to cope and ringing you with increasing frequency to come and take her home; and, on top of all this, the respite centre is now saying it cannot have Charlene with it until it gets funding for 1:1 support. This is a looming disaster for you as a family and for Charlene as an individual (as her own life is becoming increasingly restricted).

We have had a chance to talk quite a lot about this and I was able to visit Charlene in school so let's try to summarise where we are up to:

- Charlene is now 15. She has a diagnosis of ASD with severe learning difficulties.

- She has always been a person with a strong interest in the sensory world and sensory experiences.

- She has always been very active, revelling in the physical life (running, jumping, climbing, cycling).

- She has always been a visual learner and able to learn by watching. On the other hand she has always been quite resistant to direct instruction.

- She has always been very tidy.

- She is a great 'ritualiser' (her and me both!) – she quickly develops her own rules about how things are to be and then follows those quite rigidly, having difficulty in doing something familiar in a different way.

- She has always had a great sense of humour, particularly enjoying other people getting into trouble and having 'accidents' (tripping, dropping things – slapstick stuff).

What has changed over the last year is that she has started to spend more and more time on her 'obsessions' – spitting on things and wiping the spit as if to clean them and collecting any cups, bottle and cans that she sees and trying to wash them and put them away (not popular with other people when they are drinking from these things!). She is also running off the minute she is outside a confined space (she does have a very limited sense of danger). She is now spending most of her time on these cleaning and tidying activities both at home and in school. She is also increasingly resistant to being interrupted/redirected and on occasion has pushed, hit or kicked adults who have tried to intervene (this does not happen every time – sometimes she can be redirected). We are clearly in need of some kind of strategy to move this situation on in a constructive way. Here are a few thoughts.

The term 'obsession' is used rather freely around people with autism. It refers to at least three different phenomena:

1. *Obsessions...and compulsions*. Here the person engages in a behaviour repeatedly. The mood is often quite dark. The behaviour does not seem to bring any joy although there may be some relief (short term) once the behaviour is completed. Attempts to interrupt or redirect are often met by a strong surge of negative emotion, usually accompanied by behaviours such as aggression, self-injury and/or property damage. When you look at the person as a whole you usually find that he or she is not in the best of shape – he or she appears to be suffering from a more general lack of well being of which the rise in 'obsessions' is just one part.

2. *Obsessions...as passions*. Here the person has a behaviour that he or she likes to do over and over. He or she generally enjoys the behaviour – it seems to bring interest and pleasure. These individuals are in quite good shape; their well being seems intact. They do not necessarily like accepting limits, but if the limits are part of a clear structure and there is respect and time given to allowing/encouraging/developing the

interest then these behaviours can usually be limited. These kinds of 'obsessions' are often a key strength that will play an important and constructive part in the person's life (for example, being useful for a job or membership of a club or gaining access to further/higher education).

3 A *development of 2*. But taken to the point of 'addiction'. Here the person enjoys the activity but cannot get enough of it. He or she wants to do it all the time – it takes over his or her life. As the 'obsession' becomes more and more pervasive so the individual becomes more and more resistant to interruption and redirection, often developing major behavioural challenges (especially physical aggression) as a means of encouraging people to back off.

Having looked at all the information that we have about Charlene I think we are dealing with something that is more in category 3. If so we need to think about the kinds of approaches that will help us move on in a constructive way – let 'controlled drinking' be our model! I would suggest:

- We need to revamp the general activities that we offer to Charlene. We need to capture her interest and draw her attention away from an exclusive focus on cleaning, tidying and playing chase. This means revamping her 'curriculum' to focus on high impact activities – some of the ideas we came up with included cooking, structured physical exercise (obstacle courses, relay running, trampolining, climbing), new/more complex puzzles, new art/craft activities, learning a musical instrument, learning magic tricks.

- Linked to this, we need to take on board Charlene's long-standing interest in cleaning and tidying, her age (approaching adulthood) and our 'controlled drinking' approach. Thus as part of her curriculum review we should be looking to provide structured access to recycling, gardening, pressure washing, cleaning – proper, potentially vocational activities that incorporate her interests.

- At the day-to-day management level we should continue to work hard to limit her access to 'obsession' triggers such as cups, cans, plastic bottles and dirty surfaces (we will never succeed entirely with this but any limiting will help). We should structure transitions carefully so that the focus is on what she is going to not what she is stopping; and we should look at the use of high-value distracters during transitions from one place to another (for example, iPod, DS, mirror, favourite book, chewy sweets).

- We need to keep reminding ourselves about who Charlene is, what she loves, what we love about her and what supports work for her. Specifically, we need to check out that we have in place the kinds of visual supports that are central to Charlene being able to understand the world and to learn.

If we develop these action plans, I would not expect an immediate impact. All those involved need to get on the same page and work together on this – a big challenge, perhaps bigger than Charlene's challenges. But if that can be achieved, I am sure that we will begin to see progress over the next several months. If that cannot be achieved and we persist in limiting Charlene's life, excluding her and 'fighting' with her, then I fear that her 'addiction' may become a 'compulsion' as her overall sense of well being is lost. She has too many precious gifts to allow that to happen.

I hope this all makes sense and that it is of some help to you. These are just starter ideas and I am sure you will have a lot of your own to bring up and add to the mix. Please keep me posted on how things go – let's keep this conversation going.

All best wishes.

Update

Things have not gone terribly well. It has proved difficult to get all those involved to see things in the same way and to develop the kinds of action plans outlined in this letter. The family are considering a major change in service provision and are looking at the alternatives available to them.

B. Marcus (physical aggression)

Marcus is a very articulate, primary-school-age child with multiple diagnoses (see below). He has always been very controlling but this is now being expressed sometimes by serious levels of violence in the home. The picture is similar in school.

Dear _____,

It was lovely to hear from you again, but I was very concerned to hear about the increasingly frequent and severe meltdowns that Marcus is presenting at home. I think it is deeply shocking as a parent when you find yourself being punched, kicked and bitten by your nine-year-old child. I am very sorry that all of you are going through this right now. Let's see if we can make some sense of this and find a way forward.

To recap on what we know:

- Marcus is now nine and has been tagged with a variety of 'official labels' – high-functioning autism, ADHD, Asperger's syndrome.

- He has always been something of a free spirit, very controlling, only wanting to do what he wants to do and quite resistant to demands or denials of any kind.

- He is a definite thrill seeker, loving to climb, to ride his BMX to destruction and to experience the wildest funfair rides possible.

- He is quite easily distracted unless he is involved in some of his favourite hobby-type activities, such as riding his BMX, playing video games and building Lego models. On these activities he can sustain a focus of attention for extended periods (hours).

He has always had tantrums when he could not get his own way, but recently they have increased in frequency and severity and are now marked by intense anger, often to the point of verbally expressed hatred and threats towards you, his sister and other kids at school. He has on occasion used weapons such as a knife or a baseball bat to threaten you at home. You describe him as turning into a complete tyrant and this is making family life like walking on eggshells as you can never be sure when he is going to kick off. At the same time you have noticed how negative he has become about himself, belittling any achievement he makes, getting furious when he is praised, referring on occasion to his 'stupid autistic brain'.

You asked me if I had come across anything like this before. The answer is a very definite yes. It is not a presentation that you find much described in the current literature on Asperger's syndrome, but it is certainly a picture that I see quite frequently.

In terms of making sense of this we have to start by acknowledging that some of this is to do with who Marcus is and how he is...as a human being. He has always been very controlling and will likely remain so, which is not in any way a bad thing and indeed can advantage you in later life. However, this characteristic has taken a very negative and destructive turn. Your feeling is that this began when two things happened. First, Marcus moved class and changed teacher after a period of two years during which time he had had the same teacher, someone with whom he got on very well. At about the same time his sister transferred to secondary level with a scholarship to a very prestigious public school.

With the information that we have shared I am thinking that what is happening here is that Marcus has lost his sense of well being. He is increasingly dominated by negative thoughts and feelings and, in particular, he seems to have a knot of anger inside him that explodes at sometimes the smallest trigger. As well as this almost physical experience Marcus has developed a very negative view of himself and his situation, a kind of hopelessness and helplessness which for a person who likes to be in control is very scary. He is in a hole and we need to see what we can do to dig him out. I would think in terms of the following:

- Introduce into everyday life activities that specifically work to enhance mood – see if we can get him taking more physical exercise, increase the frequency of laughter (a joke book might help here), look at how you might use music in the home to impact mood, try to introduce some 'pampering' (for example, hair washing, foot and hand care) and if you have any massage therapists or cranial osteopaths nearby you might give those a try. I would also look to reducing the amount of verbal conversation at specific 'fragile times', such as in the morning before school or on return from school in the afternoon. Food and music beat conversation for short-term well being!

- I note that Marcus is on the waiting list for some kind of psychological therapy from your local Child and Adolescent Mental Health Service (CAMH). That could certainly help. But I have also found lower-tech interventions have a role to play as well. It would be good if we could bring a young man into Marcus' life, someone who was not a parent or a teacher, someone Marcus could hang out with and do things together with – a listening ear. I don't know if you have any kind of local befriending scheme, or if there is someone in your extended family (an uncle/cousin) or whether the school could do something via its pastoral care system. This kind of relationship can take the pressure off the primary relationships (parent and teacher). It gives Marcus a space where he can just be, and if he wants to talk about things then that is good but there is no pressure to do so.

- We need to think about how we can strengthen Marcus' sense of himself as a valuable person (I am avoiding the dreaded term 'self-esteem'!). Partly this is work for all of us to do (parents and school). We need to think carefully about the things that we truly value in Marcus and how we communicate to him that these are things we value. I am not much in favour of repeatedly reassuring people ('Oh you are clever, Marcus, no one can build Lego like you') as in my experience this will often trigger an argument with Marcus making a huge effort to prove us wrong. Rather I would want to put Marcus in situations where he could experience being useful. Are there clubs he could join that reflect his talents, are there chores at home that would help the running of the home, are there opportunities for him to 'volunteer' (for example, reading to the infants, helping out at a local animal rescue place)? It is the experience of doing valuable things that is more important than the verbal reassurance that you are valuable (although I would not of course ban reassurance altogether! I just think we need more than that).

So those kinds of interventions will help get Marcus experiencing a greater sense of well being. We need to talk also about the management of incidents, given the severity of the behaviours you are facing:

- You need to put up a poster or notice at home that outlines the key rules in 'our house' and how any violent incidents will be managed (i.e. you need a plan or drill, like a fire drill that you will follow when these kinds of behavioural emergency occur). The details of what such a drill might involve you will need to think about realistically, basing it on what you know about how the incidents go, the resources you typically have available for managing incidents, the constraints imposed by the house and who else is around. The key thing is to have a plan that you will try to follow and that is realistic (of course it won't be easy). Posting this up is reassuring for you and for Marcus. It is important to deal with incidents as calmly as possible, given the fraught nature of the incidents. Having a plan helps to keep you focused and lets Marcus know that you can cope. It can be very scary to feel yourself losing control and being with people who do not convey the message they can handle the situation. It leads to rapid escalation and loss of control, particularly in someone for whom control is such a central issue. If you feel that to manage incidents at home you need to get physically involved with holding or moving Marcus, then you should try to get yourselves on a course in crisis management – most special schools train their staff in this way and these kinds of training are increasingly being opened to parents, but you will need to explore the local situation where you live.

- In your management plan make sure that the decision about when to back off and reduce restrictions is one that you make. Do not get into 'bargaining' with Marcus, promising things he can have or do when he is calm – make the decisions yourself about when you judge the situation to have become safe again.

- With people who are very controlling, formal reward schemes often do not work that well. However, I would have in mind an idea of how you might positively reinforce Marcus if he starts to behave aggressively and then manages to turn it around, managing control himself by his own efforts before he has done any harm. The reward would be a one-off and a way of us acknowledging Marcus' competence and strength (see below). The development of self-regulation skills is a key part of equipping Marcus long term with the resources to manage frustration constructively, and if we can get some improvements in terms of frequency of incidents we will need to talk much more about promoting development in this area (which is something of a 'hidden deficit' for many youngsters with an ASD).

- Once an incident is finished, think about how to convey to Marcus that you are sorry about what happened, that he must have been 'under the weather', 'not quite himself' to lose control like that and how awful that must have been for him. Try not to be angry with him. You may levy consequences if that is part of your plan but do so in terms of 'following the plan' rather than 'punishing a naughty boy'. The point of this kind of reaction is to undermine the power of Marcus' behaviour, to counter the notion that violence is strength and rather to suggest it reflects a lack of something. This will also encourage Marcus to become more reflective about his feelings and behaviour, making a positive contribution to our agenda for developing self-awareness and self-regulation.

Well, I think that's as far as I can go for now. Let's keep talking until we come up with a plan that both reflects our understanding of what is going on and is workable for you all.

Keep me posted.

All best wishes.

Update

The family worked hard to put into practice some of these ideas and saw some improvement at home. However, problems arose at school (not related to Marcus) which in the end meant that a change of school was sought. This kind of upheaval inevitably sets back the kind of long-term work that is needed to help Marcus manage his feelings in less destructive ways.

C. Tyrone (verbal abuse, physical aggression, property damage)

Here again we have a young, articulate child where control issues loom large. It is a real concern that there has been so little research and discussion around this topic of control, which is at the heart of many very serious behavioural issues.

The format here is slightly different as I provide the background information separately from my letter about approaches to support as the family provided me with a lot of documentation prior to us discussing what to do.

Background

Tyrone is now seven years old. He lives with his mum and dad, two younger sisters and the family dog (!). From his first days in this world he has been quite challenging to parent – prone to a lot of negative emotions, very demanding, hard to settle, not very amenable. As he grew up he struggled to form relationships with other young children, found it hard to focus on what other people wanted him to focus on, preferred to do his own thing and had a lot of energy to burn. By the age of six he had been tagged as ADHD and Asperger's syndrome and was certainly aware that he was different from others.

His parents got in contact because they were at their wits' end about how to construct family life with Tyrone. He was very controlling, especially with his mother, wanting to determine everything she did and disrupting any attempt she made to get on with other things (telephone calls, doing things with the other kids, spending time with her husband). If he did not get his way, Tyrone would verbally abuse his mother and throw things at her, and had also on occasion slapped her round the face. She described the feelings as like being a victim of domestic abuse. Tyrone was also very controlling of other aspects of family life, constantly bossing his sisters and the dog around. At school he presented few problems, and the school had made it pretty clear that he was getting on just fine and virtually stated that the problems at home must reflect the kind of parenting that was going on.

On the other side of things Tyrone is a very clever boy, a particular whiz at computer/phone technology. He is a good reader, although it is not clear that he understands as much as he can read. He loves to help out in a way that shows him as the expert or especially competent. Although he struggles in his relationships with children of the same age, he functions well with younger children (where he could be 'in charge') and teenagers/young adults, whom he regards more as his equals.

Tyrone is a perfectionist. He is pleased to get things right but devastated if he gets things wrong or makes a mistake. The meltdowns that result from 'imperfection' can be hard to manage and add to the stress in family life.

The overall impact of this was that the parents felt that the family was disintegrating. They were well read, had tried all the things that they had been advised to do but were getting nowhere, and Tyrone was more and more in control of all aspects of family life. It is at this point that the discussion begins.

Dear _____,

Thank you for getting in touch. I understand the desperation of your feelings – these control-related issues are quite common in our field but little written or researched about. Their impact on family life can be very, very severe, as it is with you guys. It may be little comfort, but you are not alone in facing this and it is not something caused by your parenting. Parenting very controlling children is a huge challenge for any parent. These children may attract a variety of labels, and we certainly see this dynamic with children on the autistic spectrum; but we see it with other, differently labelled children as well.

So let's start with a few general points and then get on to specifics. First, let us be clear that being controlling is not in and of itself a problem. Indeed it can have many advantages later in life. It is a huge challenge to parenting (and it will be to educating – yes, it will be coming their way soon!), but remember that some of the most successful people on the planet are this way. We tend to use different terms for these adults – leaders, driven, demanding, determined, inspired, genius, relentless. Our challenge as parents is to negotiate this dynamic so that it does not do the family or the child in (which it can easily do) and enables the child to realise the positive futures that are potentially available.

Moving to the slightly more specific, you are quite right to note the huge gap between Tyrone's general intelligence and his social-emotional (im)maturity. Sometimes he is a teenager, sometimes a seven-year-old, sometimes a two-year-old; and you have to parent each one of those! What a challenge – who's in the room right now and how do I respond to that person… Am I dealing with the toddler, the seven-year-old or teenager? We cannot be one kind of parent, hence the difficulty. It gets very confusing – so interrupting your telephone conversations is a toddler behaviour, but most toddlers do not call you a f****** b**** and scream at the top of their lungs, 'I hate you' to get you off the phone. This verbal add-on makes it hard to see the toddler who is really there. So, in this example, we need to remember that you have brought up three toddlers – we need to draw on what you have learned from this. So, for now, we ignore the 'grown up' verbal abuse. We focus instead on making headway with you being able to talk on the phone without being controlled by this 'toddler'.

You also are puzzled about why Tyrone can be so meek and mild at school while being such a dominant force at home. Differences in the behaviour of children between school and home are the rule rather than the exception. Being always the same is an unusual human characteristic. It is entirely possible that such differences in behaviour at school and home reflect differences in how the children are managed. Parents can be more indulgent and less firm than teachers…or not. You may be like this and indulging Tyrone's every whim because you feel sorry for him. I am not hearing this, and there are other explanations. Something we certainly see with Asperger's children is that school is a very stressful situation. Some of them can devote a lot of effort to trying to fit in and not be noticed as different. This is a tremendous stress, not obvious on the surface at school, but pretty obvious the minute they step through the door at home after school, when they decompress big time. Some will withdraw to a quiet, dark place, some will just meltdown at the least trigger, others can only get to meltdown by 'picking a fight' (setting up a situation whereby the parent is bound to say 'No' so that they can then let rip).

We also need to take on board something that may not be immediately obvious from the way Tyrone presents himself. In the shadow of this strong, controlling, demanding, tyrannical child is a frightened, angry little boy who has no idea which way to go. So where to begin:

How can we make Tyrone feel better...generally?

We need to look at things that we can do at home to increase Tyrone's general sense of well being. Can we increase exercise, add massage components to bathing or bedtime routines, inject more humour (joke books, whoopee cushions), seed the atmosphere with calming aromas, have more pleasurable snacks? In particular, can we use these ideas to develop a transition ritual for when Tyrone goes to and comes back from school – look to decrease the amount of language and interaction at these times, increase the visual communication and incorporate some of these elements to cut into the increase in arousal at these transition times?

We also need to talk with the school about working on Tyrone's perfectionist tendencies, to develop for him some more forgiving competence. Thus we need to teach him to start evaluating his experiences in a more flexible way. At present he has two points on his scale (good–dire) – we need to move to three (good–OK–dire), and so on. We should start this work around peripheral experiences (ice creams, TV programmes, days out, lessons) before going on to more critical experiences (work at school, behaviour at home). There are books out there to help with this (the 5-point scale[1]). This work is long term, not a quick fix, but will give Tyrone a constructive resource for coping with life's ups and

---

1   Buron, K.D. and Curtis, M. (2012) *The Incredible 5-Point Scale: Assisting and Understanding Social Interactions and Controlling Their Emotional Responses.* Overland Park, KS: Autism Asperger Publishing Company.

downs and free him from the necessity of always needing the world and himself to be 'perfect'.

How can we make Tyrone feel good about himself?

Let's start with us. At present Tyrone is rather overwhelming and the negative side is prevailing. We need to step back and think – what's great about Tyrone, what do we love about him, what is there about his uniqueness to celebrate? Doing this will release us to communicate genuinely to him what we admire, respect and adore about him. More practically, we need to look for slots in his life where he is the competent one that others rely on – are there chores at home, duties at school or even volunteering opportunities where Tyrone is in control, is competent and could earn the genuine appreciation of others?

There is also an intervention that cuts across many areas and has the potential for multiple contributions. One of the developing issues for Tyrone is that he feels different from others and does not succeed in some of the social things that his age mates manage, particularly making friends. Now of course we want to continue doing all we can to equip him with the social skills that contribute to friendship, but I think we need to do more than that. Let us play to his strength of relating well to older children/teenagers/young adults. One of the problems that happens if you struggle to make friends is that your social world is dominated by control issues – you are forced back entirely on your parents and teachers, and both these relationships have a lot of control and potential conflict involved in them. If we can inject a relationship into your life that you enjoy, that has less control involved, that offers a listening ear and a bit of advice then we may kill many birds with one stone. Such a relationship may come from within the family (a young uncle or aunt, a late-teen cousin), it may come from professional resources (pastoral care at school) or it may be engineered (a buddy/coach/mentor either from an established scheme available in your area or that you engineer specifically for Tyrone). It gives Tyrone a space of social enjoyment, a space of social success, a space to talk about things he would not talk to you or his teachers about and a space for listening (control people are much more willing to listen to 'strangers' or 'experts' than they are to parents and teachers where the relationships are so contaminated by the control dynamics involved).

How do we get Tyrone to think about his difference?

I think you have already made a good start here. He responded very well to one of the books written for youngsters of his age about Asperger's. There will be other books with which you can follow this up. He may want to talk to an 'expert' – check who might be available to you locally and take soundings if Tyrone would want to do that (don't force it). Talk with the school and think about how at home we could do a group activity about what's great about me, what do I find hard, so the focus is not on Tyrone but he can see that everyone is good at some things and not at others – he is not unusual in finding that there are things he does not understand/cannot do. Again this is long-term work around the messages that everyone is a mix of competence and incompetence and that we can learn to manage some of the things that we struggle with now (you are not stuck with this forever). Asperger's must never be an excuse and we must never encourage the victim mentality – difficulties are there to be challenged and there are people with you who understand the problem and who will help you with that...and, by the way, you have some stunning capabilities and characteristics that others do not.

How do we get Tyrone to move on from how he is behaving?

Tyrone will not respond to standard interventions of having a programme drawn up for him that is 'imposed' on him. He will tend not to be much influenced by standard reward and punishment schemes. So what to do? Well, here I turn unashamedly to psychological manipulation (you are his parents – you are allowed!). Let us take a concrete example – Mum on the telephone. Our starting point is communicating to him that we are concerned a bit that he seems stuck doing things a toddler would do (be very careful here – do not use sarcasm or humiliation – it has to be a genuine, rather puzzled concern) when he has moved on so much in other areas. We can express the hope that he can get stronger on this one and move on, but do not tell him directly that he needs to move on. You can get him to check with other kids in the school what they do. We make it clear that we will manage the situation because that is what we do, but we are hopeful things can change. We need then to have our plan for managing disruption that we implement calmly. We show ourselves as in control of things. It does not matter so much what the plan is as that we stay calm and manage our frustrations. We are working here to draw Tyrone in to wanting to move on – we can ask him every so often what he thinks or he may spontaneously say he wants to do it. If we judge Tyrone is on board, we can start to work together with him on a plan – what warning he needs of a phone call, what he can do instead during that time, what he can do with his strong feelings, what length of call does he think he can manage, does he need a reward if he succeeds…or not.

Now this is just one example, but I hope it gives a sense of the general style that may be needed when working with very controlling people around behaviour change issues. It will take time because you have to get the person on board with wanting to change but this approach is more likely to succeed than getting angry, levying costs, promising rewards…but then you know all that already.

My goodness me, I have gone on for much longer than I meant to and re-reading all that it seems rather overwhelming. So we need to be realistic. Think about this. Think about the things that you can take on board right now – limit that list, do one or two things, don't take on board lots of things that you find later you can't keep up. Most of what we are talking about here needs to be sustained long term, so start small and build up. Some of the things can be helped along by others, particularly the school, so talk with people there about what they might be prepared to take on board.

This is a blueprint for a 'project' of many years. I am sure we will need to continue our conversations. If there are things that you are not clear about, that is probably because I have not made them clear, so ask me to be clearer. If there are things that you do not feel are a good fit for Tyrone and the way your family operates, then trust your judgement not mine.

I look forward to the 'next episode'.

With all best wishes.

Update

No further information was available at the time of writing this book.

D. Charlie (a danger to self and others)

This conversation is about a scenario that no family would want to face – the behaviour of their child becomes so dangerous that there is an increasing risk of police involvement and/or compulsory detention under mental health legislation. This is a scenario that some parents of young people with an ASD will find themselves facing.

It would be wrong to say that this situation is common. However, it is something that recurs regularly and needs confronting in an open and honest way. Most of the families with whom I have had these conversations have an adolescent/young adult son who is regarded as relatively 'high functioning' – that is they can talk quite well. Most of the families are not like Charlie's family and have next to no involvement from 'services'. An oft repeated scenario is that mental health services decline to be involved because this is about 'autism', and learning disability services decline to be involved because the young person is 'too able'. The situations themselves have developed over quite a long period of time (they do not happen overnight), running a deteriorating course, and at the time of discussions like this there are serious risks for all family members.

Background

Charlie is a young man of 19, living at home with his parents and two younger siblings, a brother and a sister. He has just left school and started at college doing a design technology course. Charlie has always been what my old mum would have called 'highly strung': he takes life's knocks hard and when he becomes destabilised bursts of intense anger start to occur more frequently and last longer, and this anger can be accompanied by both physical attacks on others and self-injury (banging his head against solid surfaces). Charlie is also something of an 'Eeyore' and has a tendency always to see the downside of things and to see the glass half empty rather than half full. These are long-term parts of how Charlie views the world, but now his way of expressing his propensities is moving beyond the ability of his family to keep him and themselves safe. Charlie has experienced a number of significant events in the six months running up to these conversations. He has left the special school he attended from the age of nine and began at a college where he is struggling to cope both socially and with the demands of the course itself. Over the summer a friend of his from school died unexpectedly. The recycling centre where he has volunteered for the last two years have said that they can no longer offer him work. As his anger, upset and aggression escalated his family got back in touch with me (I have had contact with them off and on over several years).

Dear _____,

Thank you for bringing me up to date with Charlie's situation and I can well imagine how on edge he is. Let's talk first about prevention, but then we need to have a much more difficult conversation. Charlie is in a down phase and so anything that we can do to boost his sense of well being at both the physical and psychological level will help – can we increase his exercise? Can we help him access 'pampering' interventions such as massage or hand or foot care? Try seeding the atmosphere with relaxing scents, given how much he likes 'jobs' see if you can find him regular jobs that involve carrying heavy items around, see if he will still use the trampoline (we can work out all the details here as we find out things that Charlie will tolerate on a regular basis). I remember also the brilliant intervention you came up with a couple of years back as a way of challenging Charlie's Eeyore/yes-but tendencies. We wanted to encourage a focus on positive thoughts and, given Charlie would start by saying something good and then qualify it with loads of negatives, you came up with asking him questions about things he liked/did well at but told him he could only answer yes or no, nothing more and every time he acknowledged a like or achievement you wrote that down on a positive thoughts list. You could also use a dream catcher and write down any hopes, dreams, positive thoughts that come up spontaneously and put them individually on a dream catcher as another way of trying to balance his internal negative bias with a concrete representation of the positives in life.

Although these interventions are important we have to talk about other matters too. You are telling me that Charlie has hit and kicked you and his siblings. In the past this would be just a one-off, but the other day he hit you several times in a sustained attack. He is also threatening to kill himself and to take a knife to college to kill some of the people there. So far you have been able to defuse these situations and Charlie has not acted on these threats. But this is serious, very serious. You are a family in crisis with the safety of you all (and others) at stake. You need to have a family discussion about crisis management – what is the plan if Charlie loses control altogether? You should agree this as a family. If you think you are going to need police support, then talk to your local police now so that they are made aware. If it is likely to involve detention under the Mental Health Act, then talk also to social services about how this happens and where Charlie would go. These are horrendous thoughts for families to have to face but if you think it will come to this be proactive, give relevant agencies a heads-up on what you are dealing with, get some idea of what might happen and do that together. The worst possibility is that we pretend this will just blow over, make no preparations and then disaster strikes and you are at the mercy of whoever turns up and what they make of the situation on the spot; and it is very likely in these circumstances that matters will end up being taken out of your hands altogether. That is much more likely to lead to very negative long-term consequences compared to where we acknowledge honestly what is going on and make plans for the worst-case scenario.

And although this all sounds horrific, bear in mind a few points. We often fear the police and assume that they will act in an unthinking heavy-handed way. However, remember that they are much better trained than most others in dealing with situations of imminent danger and can have a very calming effect because they have the confidence and skills, especially if they understand about Charlie and his issues. The second point is that your situation with Charlie is one I have seen a number of times in the last few years. These situations build up over time, with family life gradually disintegrating under the pressure and relationships fracturing as things spiral out of control. Sometimes a dramatic intervention gives everyone a chance to calm down and regroup and put together a proper long-term plan rather than muddling through day-to-day. And, finally, remember we do have a pretty good idea of the kinds of things that we can do to create a life that will work for Charlie – we may need to go through a crisis and get some breathing space in order to help everyone start to think in a more reasonable way about who Charlie is and what he needs, bearing in mind he needs a life not a placement.

Let us keep this conversation going. My thoughts are with you.

Update

Although things did not happen quite as neatly as I suggested, the elements were put in place. In the end Charlie was sectioned after he took himself off to the railway tracks and stood on the line saying he wanted to die. This intervention (his detention) did have the desired effect of enabling everyone to calm down and get on the same page with the longer-term plans for Charlie. Charlie himself settled a bit while he was away and plans were developed so that when he came out he had activities and supports better suited to his real needs. His life is moving on now, his family are intact and things are moving in a positive direction. We are not out of the woods yet and there will be ups and downs (as that is who Charlie is…life will always be a rollercoaster for him), but good things are happening and Charlie himself is now in much better shape. The violence and the threats have stopped. It is also worth noting that the police played an exemplary role in supporting this family – they 'got' Charlie and managed all their contact with him very skilfully.

E. Rudy (long-term severe self-injury and physical aggression)

This is another difficult area because it is so little discussed. Most serious behaviours can be constructively managed if we provide competent services and supports. Such services are not always available and so many issues are not properly dealt with. However, there are some individuals whom we do not fully understand and who will continue to challenge us severely over very long periods of time even if they receive good-quality, competent service support. The question arises about how we serve such individuals. The reality is that many end up still in very institutional situations, leading impoverished lives and being heavily medicated. Rudy illustrates the importance of 'standing by' people, never giving up, being open to new perspectives and understandings and being ready to respond as development of the individual continues. He also illustrates the point we return to often, about keeping to the forefront of our thinking who Rudy is and the kind of life that would work best for him rather than more 'clinical' perspectives on Rudy. The full story would also reveal the extraordinary support Rudy has received from his parents and the huge significance that their insights have played in keeping Rudy moving forward. I am hoping that one day Rudy and his family will write the story of their 'amazing journey'.

Background

These are extracts from correspondence going on over many years (15 or more). I first met Rudy when he was seven years old and living at home, attending a local special school. I was called in to provide an assessment and short-term consultation around Rudy's very serious behavioural difficulties. At the time the main concern was self-injury – Rudy would become very, very upset and bang his head hard against solid surfaces leading to bruising and cuts, fears of brain damage and damage to the visual system. At the time he had very little verbal communication skills but was highly skilled at things such as jigsaw puzzles and Lego construction. Although my direct involvement with Rudy was relatively brief, I maintained telephone and email contact with his parents over many years. They had extraordinary insights into how Rudy's mind worked and a unique ability to communicate with him. The behaviour, however, did not abate. It ran a fluctuating course but new behaviours were added – new forms of self-injury (head punching and skin gouging) and physical aggression to others (kicking, punching and biting). However, at the same time his general development proceeded both in terms of practical skills and, most importantly, in terms of his ability to communicate verbally and to understand his own feelings and needs. He moved from living at home to residential schooling and then on to an adult placement (group home) back near to his family home.

We pick up the correspondence in adult life. By this time all the behaviours are still occurring but they go through cycles, easier and more difficult phases; and they are very clearly linked to feelings of anxiety. Rudy has had many specific anxieties over the years. One very prominent concern links to his absolute passion for *The Simpsons* and his worries that past episodes will get lost by the television companies (destroyed in a fire or thrown away), that he must do something to prevent that but cannot work out what to do. The only way he found to stop the worry cycle was to smash his head up in some way. As he grew older he then started to worry about his worries – to be anxious about anxiety and to get angry that he could not get anxiety out of the world and nor could anyone else (this might make him very angry with both his staff and his family for not getting rid of anxiety and this would precipitate attacks upon them). It is also important to acknowledge that Rudy is and always has been a 'my way' kind of person – he has never been Mr Amenable!

Our first discussion comes at a time when Rudy has started to spend a lot of time doing activities that he hopes will keep the worries at bay and his parents are themselves worried about the amount of stress that he is putting himself under. At the same time they are thinking about the kind of style they should adopt with Rudy. All through his life they have been very reassuring, trying to make things right for Rudy, trying to calm him themselves, and they are wondering whether they should keep on that way or try a different tack. At this time his agency is starting to think about how to become more person-centred in its approach to supporting Rudy, given that its attempts to provide a 'placement' have not been getting very far.

Dear _____,

Great to hear from you. I am not too surprised that you feel so tired – I get tired reading and thinking about the intensity of effort that is required to keep Rudy on track. Still, I am delighted that he is continuing to move forward and that there is a future opening up for him that might be richer in possibilities.

At this stage I would not worry about him filling his time so obsessively. Distraction is a smart tactic compared to ruminating on one's worries. It will only bring him to grief if his underlying state shifts so that he cannot get away from the stress, starts to become ever more obsessive and ever more unsuccessful at relieving his anxious feelings. At that point we need to think of a way of signalling to him something along the lines of 'you are not yourself/strong right now, so we need to take over a bit and help get you back on track'. This means that we look at how *we* structure things in a slightly different way and relieve him of the burden of self-management. So instead of a single support plan, we have something along the lines of 'when Rudy is in good shape (defined) we respond in this way, when he is "wobbly" we respond in this way'...and we communicate with him and discuss with him what we are seeing and why we are doing what we are doing.

Now in answer to your specific questions, his desire to take himself off to somewhere quiet when he is feeling stressed is, again, a smart choice, and staff will need to do their risk analysis and judge the safety issues in line with their specific knowledge of Rudy. Refusing to let him have this kind of space as a blanket rule (for fear of potential self-harm) is likely to be much more dangerous than a more open, nuanced approach. And, yes, do encourage him to laugh more – schedule in laughter time (does he have a favourite comedy show? Does he respond to schoolboy jokes? There are some great books around, and remember the male sense of humour rarely progresses much from this level!).

I warmed very much to your adopting a more 'matter of fact' style with Rudy. This is something I now talk a lot about on courses that I run. With some people we need to be less emotionally engaged, less overtly anxious to get certain things to happen. We need to be more challenging, if you like, and emphasise that life is about choices – we would prefer Rudy to make good choices but we will deal effectively with whatever choices he makes. It is also about communicating that we have control of some things that Rudy wants and that he needs to deal with that reality, negotiate with us and not try to bully his way to get things. I have got quite interested in the approach called Motivational Interviewing that addresses this kind of issue, though from a perspective very different from the ones that we might be familiar with in autismland. I would push Rudy – get him involved in setting his own behavioural targets and have a ritual for 'sealing the deal' – handshake, contract signing, glass of champagne (!) – whatever you think would appeal. You might want to allow for 'lapses' in the contract and work with the idea of 'lives' or chances with a way of signalling to him when he has 'lost a life' (careful with the wording here given that Rudy can be so literal...but I know you will know how best to communicate this to him).

We then need to square this stylistic approach with what I was saying above. The style is appropriate when Rudy is strong and actively coping, but if we feel he is breaking down and coping is not succeeding any more then we shift the balance of power a little. We indicate that we will now take a bit more control but continue to keep Rudy as involved as possible in whatever decisions he is capable of making (that is, we do not take over completely but reduce the demands on him for a period of time...until he is back on track). Does this make any sense to you?

Anyway, those are my thoughts for the day.

All best wishes.

Rudy is and always has been a very intense person. Crises are readily precipitated in his life, often by his own behaviour. Yet he has continued to march forward in terms of his understanding and competence in many areas. This next brief communication picks up on that, after a recent 'crisis':

Dear _____,

Sorry for the delay in getting back to you. The situation around Rudy continues to swirl in very intense ways. But there he is, in the eye of the hurricane, continuing to move forward and produce these amazing insights. If we could focus on this core of him and not be distracted by all the other stuff, would that help I wonder? It feels like services are always 'chasing' his behaviour and emotions, quite understandably, but that means we may be missing the real issue. Not sure I am entirely clear what I mean here – shooting from the hip really. Keep me posted as and when you have time.

In the midst of all his crises Rudy's insight continued to develop and his staff grew with him. At this point he has now become able not just to identify his feelings but also work out how long it will be before he feels better (few days, end of week), what he needs to do to make that happen, including taking time away in a quiet place, communicate that to his staff who have been able to work with and accommodate this...we reflect on this:

Dear _____,

Well, never a dull moment! How fantastic that Rudy has developed this insight and been able to persuade others to accommodate his understanding. As I think I have said before, I come to see it as increasingly important that we help people not so much to understand others as to understand themselves – who they are, how they work, how they can manage that self to maximum advantage so that their lives can progress and not be destroyed. I look forward to hearing if more is to come from Rudy in that respect. And for us outsiders it changes the agenda big time.

Take care now. Best wishes to you all.

And picking up on this last communication:

Dear _____,

I have been thinking about our last communication and wondering how Rudy's self-awareness has grown in the way it has. Did he just get older, did he have a flash of insight or did he finally take on board some of the input that he received about this? That is, if you had not kept challenging him in this way over the years, would he have stayed just the same? Is his progress a late response to input that has been ongoing over many years? This is a very important question, generally: the idea of 'sleeper interventions' or 'delayed responses'. Mostly, when we evaluate therapeutic or educational practices, we look for some fairly immediate response to our efforts. However, we do understand that in child development some parenting strategies, such as giving explanations to young children about their behaviour, have no short-term impact (they still get up to no good) but have a very important longer-term impact (years later they become more self-directed compared to children not given such explanations). In autismland we tend to view behavioural work as a mix of therapy and education and to focus on immediate returns. However, it could be that some of our most important interventions have no immediate impact but may impact further down the line. This has major implications for expectations, evaluation, staff training, maintaining interventions...and so on and so on.

All thoughts gratefully received.

So Rudy, now a young adult, still has his ups and downs but also continues the long march forward...we will leave (most of) the last words to his parents:

[Rudy] has exceeded our expectations from when you first met him in many ways regarding insight, awareness and communication; however, he still continues to challenge and give cause for concern. He finds it very difficult still to communicate his needs/difficulties understanding verbally to another person in the moment so to speak. He still needs someone to be with him who really understands him as an individual... I would still not consider being with him without additional support and he does have 1:1 support at all times as part of his entitlement.

So behaviourally Rudy can still present serious challenges. Recently he has also developed a medical condition that threatens to have very serious impacts on his life. However, his overall progress means that his service agency is now planning to move him on to having his own flat, something Rudy is very keen on. But get this:

[Rudy] invited us on holiday with him and his key worker in a cottage near Rutland – which was a first – he paid! Suddenly we felt in a whole new ball game which was interesting as the power dynamics had changed. We had a really great time. We (Mum and Dad) were surplus to requirements and trailed around feeling like a spare leg as he has such a close relationship with [key worker], and we felt quite sad at not being wanted any more although we consoled ourselves that this was inevitable and to be expected, and we were pleased for both of them but at the same time we have to confess it was quite liberating. However, Mum got an unexpected reward as we were about to get in our respective cars and depart, as Rudy suddenly locked his arms around her in the biggest and first spontaneous hug she has ever had, and said he didn't want Mum to go – not that she could anyway – his arms measure 15 inches around their biceps – so she just had to stand there until he was ready to let go. [Key worker] was so surprised and said she had never quite realised the depth of his feelings in regard to us, and managed to get lots of photos. It was a very special moment for all of us. We felt very touched and if we are honest quite smug about it after what she said! What a treat for all of us – such joy.

Section comments

The reader will see from this section some vivid illustrations of the problems some families face and how to construct a psychological view of these problems in a way that will lead on to practical help. Sometimes these ideas were taken on board, implemented and made a difference. But also illustrated is the oft-repeated scenario where a shared view is not developed, shared action plans are not implemented and nothing changes (or things get worse). The point here is not that my ideas are necessarily 'right' but that help for the person with developmental disabilities is dependent on the people without identified disabilities developing a shared view and shared action plans. In so far as they fail to do this then help is actively denied and serious situations remain intractable. In this sense the behaviour of people without identified disabilities is just as problematic and challenging as the behaviour of the person with identified disabilities.

Section 4

Epistles on challenging orthodox thinking

This part of the book is rather different from the others. It takes areas of practice that have the status of 'received wisdom' and challenges both the assumptions of and the effectiveness claimed for these practices. The aim here is to illustrate a broader point for parents, not just raise questions about these two specific areas of practice. I am hoping to encourage parents to be sceptical but in a constructive way. As they go along, parents will meet many experts and be told many things that are supposed to be 'good for their child'. They may well be given very different, even contradictory, advice by different people. Then there is the internet – that glorious invention that empowers us so often with vital information but also encourages a fatal confusion of fact and opinion. The internet is full of loud voices proclaiming their opinion as the 'one right way'. All this information and advice can be very confusing for parents. There is a temptation either to ignore it all or to join one particular school of thought and become disciples of the 'one right way', whether that is Son-Rise, Applied Behaviour Analysis, elaborate 'detoxification' approaches, restrictive diets, etc., etc.

The truth is that matters are too messy for false dichotomies such as 'don't believe anything you are told' and 'only believe what guru X tells you'. The most constructive way forward for a family is to keep an open but questioning mind – listen, question, look for the evidence behind opinions offered and choose on that basis the things that feel right for your child. 'True believers' will often sneer at this approach as 'eclecticism'...but then that is just an opinion and there is no evidence that 'eclecticism' leads to worse outcomes than following the 'one true path'!

So we will try to illustrate how to make use of constructive scepticism by examining sensory integration approaches and residential schooling for children and young people with significant developmental disabilities.

A. Sensory integration – brain changer or licence to twiddle?

Quite a lot of children with developmental disabilities, including but not exclusively those with an ASD, engage in high-rate, repetitive physical movements that appear to others to serve no social purpose. These might be movements of just the body itself – hand flapping, spinning, bouncing, head weaving, rocking. The movements can also involve objects – light switches turned on and off, doors opened and closed, items waved back and forth. These behaviours have been thought to achieve some interesting sensory experience for the person and have often been labelled 'self-stimulatory'. They were the focus of quite a lot of research from the late 1950s through the 1960s, research now largely forgotten. This research did indeed indicate that some of these behaviours were a form of 'self-entertainment', but that others were a form of 'stress reduction', a means of bringing the person to a calmer state, a mantra if you will.

There was a second set of behaviours that were noticed and that seemed to have a sensory basis. This involved the triggering of extreme emotional upset by what others would have regarded as ordinary everyday sensory inputs – sounds such as lawn mowers or babies crying, textures and colours of food, crowded fast-moving environments, smells of various kinds (a lot of individual differences with no common underlying theme, other than they were intensely unpleasant experiences for the individual in question). Aversive reactions to sensory experiences are fairly universal in human beings, but the significance of these issues, their impact on everyday life and social functioning, seemed much greater for those identified with an ASD.

The current era of taking a more positive view about people with developmental disabilities began in the mid to late 1950s. At the start of this period the repetitive behaviours were viewed either as 'self-stimulatory' and as interfering with more 'appropriate' learning or as 'symptoms' of an underlying illness/disorder. Both these views led towards the idea that these behaviours should be reduced or suppressed. The aversive reactions to sensory stimuli were noted but largely ignored in this early period, although there was a perfectly applicable model being developed elsewhere in behaviour therapy – the phobia model. Phobias affect a large number of people and involve a very strong emotional reaction to specific stimuli that trouble others not at all (heights, spiders, sharp objects, blood, lifts, flying and so on). The model developed saw phobias being based on anxiety, and the 'new treatment' meant finding ways of reducing anxiety in the presence of the phobic stimuli.

Two important developments occurred subsequently. One was the steady stream of autobiographical accounts that emerged from some of the more verbally empowered people on the autistic spectrum. Many of these accounts emphasised strongly the sensory and perceptual difficulties faced by the individual and gave as much prominence to these challenges as to difficulties with social understanding and communication. This stood in contrast to the accounts of practitioners and researchers (outsiders), who were much more focused on the social and communication problems. The second development, linked to the first, was a move towards more acceptance of things such as autism as a 'way you were' rather than a 'treatable illness', which increased tolerance for some differences that were not apparently socially destructive. This shift towards a more empathic-acceptance stance opened the way both to greater tolerance and to more detailed exploration of the causes of these differences – that is, we became interested to understand the way different minds work as opposed to suppressing behaviour.

Amongst the impacts of these changes was a renewed interest in what was quite an old proposition developed by an occupational therapist called Jean Ayres, who wrote in the early 1970s about children who had difficulty 'integrating' sensory experiences. These ideas linked the repetitive sensation-seeking behaviours and the aversiveness of other sensory-perceptual experiences as part of a single difficulty, reflecting in turn an underlying neurological problem in the areas of the brain charged with analysing and responding to the sensory world. Occupational therapy is a splendid profession and very much oriented to practical help, so of course Jean Ayres was not just going to 'theorise' but developed a whole range of fun activities that it was hoped would improve the brain's ability to handle the sensory/perceptual world – so called Sensory Integration Therapy (SIT). In the last 20 or so years such sensory integration work has spread like wildfire, certainly in the USA and UK, and now many developmentally disabled, particularly autistic, children either receive sessions of SIT or have specific sensory activities (sensory diet) woven into their school and home lives. In addition, this growing interest in sensory issues encouraged the development of specialist facilities, such as the often high-priced sensory rooms where children go for sessions/lessons to experience and learn control of a range of visual, auditory and tactile stimulation. Such activities are often (not always) experienced positively by the children themselves. As anyone involved in the autism field will recognise, having activities that you can do together with a child that are fun and enjoyable is a huge bonus in and of itself, irrespective of whether it leads to some kind of enhanced brain functioning around sensory integration. There is also a more hidden plus. Ideas of sensory integration encourage us to take a more empathic view of the other, to strive to understand that the things others observe as 'odd', 'dysfunctional', 'pointless' have a logic, a logic that reflects a difference that we should try to make sense of. This empathic stance is absolutely central to driving forward good practice and is to be contrasted with more judgemental/ pathological views that see the experience of the other as either 'challenging' or reflecting some underlying illness that has to be 'cured', thus dismissing the personal relevance of what is going on.

So I have to declare myself as starting from a position of being something of a fan for sensory integration work. But I do have concerns. There are what we might call the academic concerns. There is little evidence for specific underlying neurological differences that link to these areas of sensory functioning. There is little evidence that Sensory Integration Therapy makes any measurable difference to the child's longer-term functioning in this area. There is no automatic reason to assume that 'sensation seeking' and 'sensory defensiveness' are part of the same issue. The predominance of the sensory integration model has also served to crowd out alternative views that might have considerable merit

– for example, linking the 'stress reduction' work of the late 50s to early 60s with the unfolding developmental psychology of 'self-regulation' gives a quite different take on 'sensory defensiveness' with quite different implications. The issue from this perspective is how to teach the child to recognise and manage stressful environmental events rather than massaging his or her brain in to 'normal' functioning. Another plausible and interesting view, little considered now, is to link 'sensation-seeking' behaviours to addiction, building on the small amount of research linking some forms of self-injury to a mechanism for releasing internal opiates. This again takes one in completely different directions (managing withdrawal, building alternative experiences/opportunities). I am not saying that these alternative views are right or better than a sensory integration perspective. But they are deserving of as much consideration and themselves in need of further research, and I emphasise them here to point out that our current views and received wisdom are not necessarily correct. Fashion is not the same as progress.

There is also a more urgent, practical concern. As a psychologist, I am continuing to see some very challenging adolescents/young adults who spend a lot of time engaged in the repetitive, apparently sensation-seeking behaviours. They can become very aggressive when you try to interrupt these behaviours and are very resistive to efforts directed at teaching social or other skills. They appear to be 'free running'. At one level 'leaving someone be' to 'dance to their own tune' might seem like a kind and morally agreeable thing to do (to stop trying to control people all the time, to respect their difference). But in reality there is an unfolding disaster. 'Free runners' end up being impossible to live with in a family home and impossible to teach in a local school. Their resistiveness increases over time and they drift towards ever more restrictive environments and interventions without any noticeable gain in happiness or life satisfaction. This not uncommon scenario raises a question for me: are we encouraging children to become free running by emphasising so much the importance of sensory work and allowing more and more time to be devoted to sensory activities that have a minimal social component, especially from an early age (sensory integration work often starts from young)? It is this potential downside that concerns me much more than the academic arguments. Does what looks like a benign intervention have a hidden cost...for some people? Should we be considering this when we are making decisions about what supports we regard as appropriate for a child? There is no hard research evidence for my concerns. My judgement may be in error. But it indicates the need to think carefully about practice in this sensory area and not to accept uncritically what have now become very widespread practices.

This is a book for parents and it is of no help just to raise an alarm like this and leave parents to it. I will try to spell out what I see as the practical implications for families and the decisions that they need to make about the supports that are right for their individual child:

- If you are offered or are seeking sensory integration work for your child, discuss with the therapist what you think it will achieve and how will you know if it is working – what will be the differences that you will notice if the therapy is working and, roughly, how long before you begin to see these differences. And if it seems right for your child *go for it!* But monitor the situation to see if the expected outcomes are being achieved.

- If you decide to get involved, keep a watch on whether some of the interventions mean an increase in the time that the child spends on self-directed sensory activities and a decrease in the time spent on activities that involve engagement with others.

Sessions of SIT with a directing therapist are not a problem; but sessions in 'sensory rooms' or with 'sensory diet' activities can be, if they come to occupy significant portions of the day and come at the expense of social engagement. Social engagement is absolutely crucial, and as long as we remain able to engage and teach the child, no problem. But if the child spends ever more time on self-directed sensory activity and is increasingly resistant to engagement with others, then we have a problem.

- Do not look to sensory interventions to sort out the kinds of social problems that arise from specific sensitivities (e.g. attacking babies who cry, running impulsively when a leaf blower starts up). Think of how to build directly better coping capacities (can we teach the child to control the emotional response, to calm, can we teach the child something to do instead of attacking, running?).

- Remember that there are other approaches. In particular, some sensory reactions can be treated in the way we treat phobias in other people, by the process of 'desensitisation'. As this is quite a technical procedure, the support of a qualified behaviour therapist would be needed for this.

- It is also important to note that an increase in sensitivity, a reduction in tolerance achieved previously, can indicate a declining sense of well being, which then needs to become itself the target for practical work. Well being is a very major issue in the lives of us all and many people with developmental disabilities are vulnerable to experiencing significant and sustained loss of well being.

So sensory work can be great; but it is not the only way and has potential costs as well as potential benefits.

Returning to more general, 'academic' concerns, the present discussion indicates a need for the academic/research community to start taking more interest again in repetitive movements and sensory aversiveness. There was a very active interest in the 50s and 60s but since then the area has been 'turned over' to sensory integration as the research community has shifted its efforts to cognitive and communication issues or genetic issues. The last named, ironically, reinforces the contention here. Genetic studies tend to indicate that repetitive behaviours form a very distinct cluster quite independent of the other areas that we associate with autism. If we can renew this interest perhaps we can come up with some more soundly based advice to parents. At present, parents have to make important decisions about the supports for their children with very little factual information about the implications/likely outcomes of these decisions; and often with very little knowledgeable professional support. In the absence of solid evidence, critical thinking becomes essential.

B. Boarding schools in the UK – a solution for difficult problems or a British disease?

In the array of services available in the UK to children and young people with developmental disabilities there continues to be an option for residential schooling of some sort. These schools may operate on a weekly, termly or in some cases a 52-week basis. This is a long-standing part of the UK system, but it has to be understood as connected to our culture – it is not an option necessitated by our understanding of developmental disabilities. There are plenty of places in the world that do not have this as a service option paid for out of the public purse.

Although this is not primarily a historical analysis I think it is helpful to have some perspective on how this option has developed in this cultural context. The UK, like many other parts of the world, has a long-standing and thriving private education sector which includes many boarding schools. Some of these schools go back long before Victorian times, although we associate their rise to prominence with that era. Thus sending children away to school has long been part of how the UK has provided education, particularly for the privileged (or 'special' as we might call them). The Victorians were equally keen on sending away other 'special' groups – some of these institutions were regarded as asylums where those sent could get away from the pressures of ordinary life (including appalling social conditions arising during the Industrial Revolution) as a means of helping them regain their equilibrium and personal functioning. Others had a more overtly educational function, but with the idea, again, that good educational outcomes could only be achieved by removing the child from adverse conditions. Thus many of these institutions grew up in rural locations, far away from the disease, disruption and social dysfunction of the cities that were expanding so rapidly at the time. Sending children away has had therefore a long history associated with an ethos of assisting development and/or recovery.

Interestingly, the subsequent history of the private schools has been rather different to that of the other institutions for the more needy. Of course, private schools go through phases and sometimes get into difficulties, but they have retained overall a reputation for excellence in terms of educational outcomes. Not so the asylums and special schools, which lost their early optimism for what could be achieved, became overcrowded and underfunded and drifted towards a culture of hopelessness, containment, neglect and overt abuse. This era culminated in the mid 20th century with a series of scandals both in the UK and USA about conditions in these institutions. This led to a reorientation of social policy for those with developmental disabilities towards 'community care' and an end to sending people away.

However, residential schools in the UK, unlike the long-stay hospitals for the 'mentally handicapped', have survived this general policy shift. They offer an alternative that families will consider, either because they initiate this interest themselves or because it is recommended to them. This alternative is now most often considered when the child or young person is presenting behavioural challenges that local services are struggling to address adequately. What might be the merits of such provision? How do parents assess whether this is an option that they might want to consider?

There will be a number of rationales put forward in favour of a residential school option. There will be mention of 'structure', that these schools provide a structure that goes across the whole day/week, that they provide this in a way that is very difficult for families to do and that this level of structure is an advantage for children and young people with developmental disabilities. Linked to the notion of structure is the argument for 'consistency', that residential schooling can provide a consistency of approach that is very difficult for families and local schools to achieve. Structure and consistency are seen as a key to resolving some of the more challenging behaviours, with an implication that the causes for these behaviours lie in lack of structure and consistency. There may also be put forward an argument that residential schools develop a very high level of special expertise, bringing in additional relevant professionals not always available locally – that is, they are 'centres of excellence'.

Let us consider some of these arguments. First, let us examine the idea that the major behavioural challenges presented by people with developmental disabilities arise because of lack of structure and consistency. There is absolutely no evidence for such an assumption –

behavioural challenges arise for multiple, interacting causal contributors and lack of structure and consistency are not prominent among these. Now it may be that structure and consistency will help when we try to drive forward constructive responses to behavioural challenges, but here again their role can be overplayed compared to the role of well-thought-out, competently delivered interventions based on an understanding of what factors are driving the behaviour. Even if we accept that structure and consistency are an advantage, there is still the question as to whether residential schools excel at such virtues. Think about the shift patterns that are needed to sustain a residential school, particularly the termly or 52-week options; think of the number of people that are involved in each individual child; then factor in staff turnover, likely to be quite high on the residential care staff side; and understand that many of the staff involved on a moment-to-moment basis are untrained and unqualified – when these factors are taken into account it is hard to see how the level of structure and consistency in residential schools is necessarily any greater than could be provided by more locally crafted options.

There is one other factor that nobody will discuss but that anybody who has been involved in this service option will know about. In many residential schools the teaching staff and residential staff do not get on well together, with relations that can be distant and disengaged or sometimes better described as 'warfare'. Teaching staff are qualified, comparatively well paid, have very good terms and conditions, including access to training, and have quite high social status. Those working on the residential side often are not qualified, are poorly paid, have to work all the unsocial hours (evenings and weekends) with limited access to training, and have relatively poor social status. To manage this situation so that 'structure and consistency' are achieved requires organisational development and managerial skills of the highest degree; and even then it is an uphill struggle.

Finally, there is the notion of 'centres of excellence', the fact that a residential school might develop specialised expertise and attract in a range of professionals that means that the child has access to competence that is difficult to achieve elsewhere. There is no evidence that residential schools are advantaged in this respect. Some may achieve this status, but so do some locally based services. Indeed, our single biggest problem in the UK is the huge variability in quality provision of all kinds for people with developmental disabilities. For families this is the real nightmare, that you cannot guarantee level of competence in service provision available to you whether local or far away. It may be good, it may be bad; it is something of a lottery. Even if you have one very good service available to you that does not guarantee that the rest of the service provision is of the same standard – having a great early intervention service does not mean that you have great schools or adult services or good behavioural support services.

So the usual justifications for sending away children and young people with developmental disabilities seem based on assumptions for which there is no evidence. Does that mean that residential schooling has no place in our service provision and should be eliminated in the way that we eliminated 'hospitals for the mentally handicapped' as a service option? Probably not; but I think that we have to step back and instead of relying on assumptions about structure and consistency and special expertise we need to look at what traditional private schools have to offer. Of course they offer many things but some of the advantages most relevant to the present discussion are:

- They often provide increased access to educational inputs. The schooling time may be longer (including, for example, longer days and Saturday morning school), the class sizes smaller.

- They are often able to provide a range of sports and leisure activities that no family could provide. They offer the child an overall quality of life that is hard to achieve on a local basis with just your own family resources.

- They can shelter a child from a range of disruptive family influences. Thus children of those in the armed services may be protected from the frequent moves and upheavals that can be part of that life. Children living among conflicted families or dysfunctional influences can obtain a degree of protection (that aspect of the novel *Jane Eyre* is interesting to consider).

- And, yes, these are places that are highly structured and a large amount of the child's time is occupied in scheduled activities (lessons, chapel, sports, homework, trips).

- Teachers work across all environments (house leaders are teachers, boarding houses also have assigned tutors) – there is no rigid demarcation between teaching and care staff.

These factors translate into a starter list of questions that a family can use to reflect on the potential advantages of a residential school that is being offered:

- Does the school I am being offered provide more time in education than my child currently receives?

- Does the school offer my child an overall quality of life that we simply could not manage with our own family resources?

- Will the school provide my child with a safe space, a relief from some of the pressures around him or her? This is a particularly sensitive issue for families as it means facing some very painful questions. But there are times when the pressure on families is so intense that the family may be going under and there is a downward spiral of challenging behaviour interacting with family stress and exhaustion levels that requires an intervention to save all family members.

- Will my child spend more time in scheduled activities than he or she does currently and would this sort of structure suit my child? Not every child with developmental disabilities does best when his or her time is fully structured; it is a question of individual differences, just like for any other child.

So these questions will help a family get started on deciding whether a residential option might be one to consider for their son or daughter.

These are quite general considerations. If a residential school potentially offers these advantages, then this will be followed up by visit(s) to school(s). How as a parent do you know what to look for when visiting a school, to get a sense of whether this is right for your son or daughter? Here are a few tips:

- Look through the paperwork on the school. Do not believe all that you read but extract from it a number of things that you will expect to see on your visit based on what the school says it does…and look out for those things on the visit.

- See if the principal/head seems to know the children and staff and interacts easily with them.

- As you walk round, see if the pupils you observe are spending most of their time in purposeful activities.

- Chat to staff, see if they can describe well what they are trying to achieve by what you see them doing and note if they seem interested or excited by what they are doing.

- Find out if teaching staff work across all hours of the school, putting in time at evenings and weekends.

- Ask questions about the range of experience that staff have and the issues that they find most challenging and see how that maps on to your child and his or her needs and issues.

- If the school is claiming to have specific expertise in behavioural work, ask for specific examples. You can also use the more detailed guidelines to be found in the Appendix.

Now of course no one school will tick all the boxes – there is no perfect place. But at least these questions will help a family decide whether a residential option might work for their child and for them as a family; and whether a particular residential school is likely to deliver on the outcomes that are most relevant to the family.

As well as helping families evaluate whether residential schooling is right for them, I hope also that this discussion will stimulate a reconsideration of what residential schooling is for. As long as we think of residential schooling as a dumping ground for the dysfunctional, 'special places' for congregating the behaviourally challenging, we will repeat the errors and abuses of the past and present – we will continue to provide services that by their very nature are disaster prone. We need to reject the historical stream of 'therapeutic removal' and refocus on the stream of 'educational excellence'. Then, maybe, we can retain residential schooling as a positive option in our service provision rather than a fall-back option when all else fails.

A few last thoughts

I retired from active clinical practice in September 2011, 40 years on from qualifying as a clinical psychologist in the UK. A very large part of my career has been focused on the needs of people with pervasive developmental disabilities of many types, particularly on the needs of those who present to us with significant behavioural challenges. I have worked in mental handicap hospitals, special schools, specialist assessment and treatment units, day centres, residential homes of many kinds and with families. I have worked as a practitioner in the UK, California and Singapore and taught in many parts of the world. I have had a wonderful career and enjoyed all the many opportunities that have come my way (well, most of them anyway!). But of all the work that I have done it is the work with families that remains closest to my heart.

The family is the primary influence on the child and remains at the centre of the support for that child. I understood early on how much we as professionals depended on families persisting with the challenging job of parenting for good outcomes to be achieved for the child. I was stunned to learn of the real world of such parenting, and these insights become particularly vivid when you work with families in their own homes and see what goes on, an opportunity I have had often in my career. I learned an enormous amount from the families I have worked with, both in terms of attitude and resilience and in terms of practical solutions to everyday problems. Of course, not all families are great. There are dysfunctional people who are parents, there are destructive parents and complete lunatics. But as I point out when teaching in this area, in my experience these rates of dysfunctionality, destructiveness and lunacy are no higher among parents of children with developmental disabilities than they are among people paid to provide services to people with developmental disabilities; indeed, I would suggest they are significantly lower. Sadly, research evidence in this area is somewhat lacking!

So looking back I feel very grateful for the opportunities that I have had for working with parents. I have gained an enormous amount and I only hope that I have been able to give as much to the families as I have got from them. This book comes partly from a wish to say thank you. But more than that, it is based on my work with families that I have seen/been involved with and that I hope I have been helpful to, in at least some cases. I would also hope therefore that the book would be of some small help to the families that I have never seen nor will see in the future.

Which takes me to more personal considerations. In my extended family we have a child with Down's syndrome and a child severely impacted with an ASD. We have two young sets of parents who are doing the extraordinary things that families do to bring up these youngsters, both very challenging but in very different ways, so that the best life possible is achieved. I would hope that the book will be of some small use to them on the journey that is unfolding before them.

But in among the warm fuzzy feelings are feelings of anger. When I first started my career we had some understanding of the challenges that parents face as they go about the process of bringing up their child with a developmental disability. That understanding developed rapidly and it became clear quite early on what kinds of supports families would need to manage these challenges to parenting in a constructive way. It was certainly not rocket science – some practical help at home, ready access to competent advice about specific problems, ready access to a knowledgeable, listening ear to relieve stress and to help the family problem solve. Some progress was made initially. But it is perfectly clear now that this ball has been dropped. Just taking the last 20 years I have had the opportunity to engage with hundreds, perhaps thousands of families and with very few exceptions all are struggling to access the kinds of basic family support services that we have known for decades would make a difference to the quality of their lives. I am angry about that, very angry. This book is a small contribution to families but it is no substitute for proper, locally available, competent family support services. While we have done much to improve other services for children, young people and adults with developmental disabilities I feel that we have shamefully neglected their families, the very people on whom the children most depend and the very people on whom we as professionals most depend for our own effectiveness. If someone who is a policy maker should happen to pick up and read this book, I hope that it might trigger the understanding that we must do better, much better for the families with whom this book is concerned.

Appendix

Constructive behavioural support
Service evaluation guide

This guide is Appendix 3 in the book *Behavioural Concerns and Autistic Spectrum Disorders* (John Clements and Ewa Zarkowska, 2000, Jessica Kingsley Publishers). It is based on Chapter 14 in that book and reading that chapter would help make better sense of the rating scale reproduced here. This evaluation guide is a way of looking at the strengths and needs of a service in terms of doing competent behavioural support. It is not a comprehensive guide to service evaluation!

Key areas of service functioning are rated using a scale with a 5-point range – this is just to make it easier to 'see at a glance' where the strengths and needs lie. No detailed interpretation can be made of exact scores. Nor is it necessary to decide on an exact score – if you want to rate between the numerical anchor points, feel free!

For the first ten rating areas the anchor points are defined as follows:

1. No evidence of this

2. Some, but not much, evidence of this

3. Some evidence of this

4. Clear evidence of this

5. Very clear evidence of this

For the 11th rating area (staff turnover) the points are defined on the scale itself.

Rating areas

A general philosophy that is respectful and inclusive

1   2   3   4   5

A track record of working with significant behaviours

1   2   3   4   5

Knowledge about autism or a commitment to learn

1   2   3   4   5

Generally well organised

1   2   3   4   5

A high level of structure

1   2   3   4   5

Use of visual supports for informative communication

1   2   3   4   5

The service is oriented to quality of life, not just behaviour

1   2   3   4   5

There is a coherent approach to working positively to reduce behaviours causing justifiable concern

1   2   3   4   5

There is a coherent, well-thought-out approach to managing dangerous incidents

1   2   3   4   5

The style is collaborative rather than authoritarian

1   2   3   4   5

Staff turnover is

1	2	3	4	5
>65% pa	50–65% pa	35–50% pa	20–35% pa	<20% pa

INDEX